Praise for *Listful*

"Building and maintaining an 'external brain' for navigating our world is critical for a sustainable lifestyle. Paula Rizzo has written a fun and useful manifesto for off-loading the jobs of remembering and reminding to free up your head's bandwidth to be focused on more meaningful stuff."

—David Allen,
international bestselling author of *Getting Things Done:
The Art of Stress-Free Productivity*

"There's something so gratifying about writing out a list and scratching tasks off. *Listful Thinking* incorporates list making at work, home, and play so you can be less overwhelmed and enjoy your life."

—Julie Morgenstern,
productivity expert and *New York Times* bestselling author
of *Time Management from the Inside Out*

"Those of us who love making lists have been waiting for a terrific book like *Listful Thinking* to feed our obsession. It's practical, funny, and thought-provoking, and will inspire readers to use list making themselves—both to get more done and have more fun."

—Gretchen Rubin,
author of the #1 *New York Times* and international bestseller
The Happiness Project

"Paula Rizzo offers the antidote to the 'busier than thou society' with thoughtful, practical advice on how to make to-do lists truly work. Her straightforward and practical approach is helpful in moving us toward managing our tasks rather than our anxiety about managing our tasks. A must-have for the list maker in all of us."

—Mary Carlomagno,
author, organizer, speaker, and owner of orderperiod.com

"Making lists has turned my life around. As a fan of Paula Rizzo's blog List Producer, I will be using her *Listful Thinking* as a part of my daily routine for getting things done!"

—Reeda Joseph,
author of *Girlfriends Are Lifesavers*

Listful
Thinking

Listful
Thinking
USING LISTS *to be* MORE PRODUCTIVE, HIGHLY SUCCESSFUL *and* LESS STRESSED

by Paula Rizzo

Foreword by Julie Morgenstern

VIVA
EDITIONS

Published in the United States by Viva Editions, an imprint of
Start Midnight, LLC, 609 Greenwich Street, Sixth Floor,
New York, New York, 10014.

Printed in the United States.
Cover design: Scott Idleman/Blink
Text design: Frank Wiedemann

First Edition.
10 9 8 7 6 5 4 3 2

Trade paper ISBN: 978-1-63228-003-9
E-book ISBN: 978-1-63228-009-1

Library of Congress Cataloging-in-Publication Data

Rizzo, Paula.
 Listful thinking : using lists to be more productive, successful and less
stressed / Paula Rizzo. -- First Edition.
    pages cm
  ISBN 978-1-63228-003-9 (paperback) -- ISBN 978-1-63228-009-1 (eBook)
 1. Motivation (Psychology) 2. Time management. 3. Stress management.
4. Success. I. Title.
 BF503.R59 2015
 650.1--dc23
                              2014023104

This book is dedicated to my mother,
who taught me to find happiness in my own backyard
and always to go after my dreams—
no matter how many lists I had to make to reach them.

Table of Contents

Foreword

Not everyone is born with an organizing gene like Paula Rizzo. I certainly am not one of them. You may not guess this about me but my first love was not order—it was chaos. I was a creative, right-brained person who thrived in the unpredictability and spontaneity of the theater. I was an actress, a dancer, and a director, and I always admired those who "had it together." I was just not one of them.

Being disorganized kept me in a steady state of stress. No matter what I was doing, I was always worried about what I might be forgetting. I had a constant tape going around in my head of things I needed to remember. That loop kept me from ever being in the moment. Every tenth thought would inevitably be, "One day I'll get organized." But the truth is, getting organized terrified me.

I thought that becoming orderly would squelch my creativity and dampen my fun, spontaneous personality. I craved being more productive and organized but I didn't want to become boring. And then I had a breakthrough.

When my daughter, Jessi, was born, my world changed forever. One day I missed the opportunity to take her for her first walk, because she had fallen back asleep by the time I'd finished gathering items for the diaper bag. I realized that I needed to get my act together for her sake. Living in chaos worked when I was the only one who was impacted, but now I had a little human being I was responsible for.

So I decided to get organized even if it would diminish my creativity. I started by making a LIST of everything that belonged inside that diaper bag—so whenever there was a chance to go on an outing, I could quickly assess if anything was missing and restock that bag in an instant. Never again would my child miss an opportunity in life because I wasn't ready. That diaper-bag list was my start, and it felt so good, I began tackling other areas of my life from there. I created a LIST of every area in my life I wanted to organize, and I tackled them one by one. And, as I got organized, an interesting thing happened.

Rather than squelching my creativity, my actions felt liberating. I felt clear, confident, centered, and on top of my game. I was in control. All my ideas were in one place and I could actually take action on them. Everything I needed was at my fingertips and that sense of achievement empowered me to be even more inspired and resourceful.

I was able to be both—organized AND creative. So I set out to help people who had resisted order as I had for years. I truly understand what it means to freeze up at the idea of making a to-do list. But fear not friends—the LIST is a great starting point to begin taking control. With all of your ideas captured, it FREES you to make choices, to focus on what is MOST important, and not get sidetracked with random, small distractions that have nothing to do with what matters.

Here is a short LIST of everything that's GREAT about lists:

- Alleviate anxiety and worry that you might be forgetting something

- Enable you to focus on DOING rather than REMEMBERING

- Allow you to focus on what really matters (and get rid of what doesn't)

- Position you to delegate more easily (just pluck something off the list for a willing helper)

- Fuel your sense of accomplishment when you cross things off

- Automate key functions in your life—which makes your life easier!

As a reformed disorganized person I can tell you—it is lovely on the other side. When I met Paula we squealed about organizing bookshelves and that amazing feeling you get when you cross something off your to-do list.

But Paula and I are different. She has always captured her to-dos in a notepad the second they jump into her head and she has always filed her bills alphabetically. But that's the beauty of list making. It will help anyone—no matter if you're a productivity junkie or a more right-brained, creative type.

We are all different and I'm all about empowering people with the right tools to get and STAY organized. And Paula does just this in *Listful Thinking*. Learning to really use a to-do list to your advantage is one of the greatest organizational lessons you'll get.

Sure, I've been dubbed the "queen of putting people's lives

in order" but I'm still not perfect. As I tackle new challenges and projects, or when my workload swells and it feels like there is too much on my plate, there are days that feel chaotic. But there's always a list to pull everything together, and bring me back to center. There is always something to learn when it comes to boosting your productivity, efficiency and success and thankfully Paula has written *Listful Thinking* to guide us.

Just start small—all it takes is one list to liberate you.

Julie Morgenstern
Bestselling author of *Time Management from the Inside Out* and *Organizing from the Inside Out*

Hi. My name is Paula Rizzo, and I have glazomania. According to Dictionary.com, this condition is a passion for making lists. At Encyclo.co.uk, it is defined as "an unusual fascination with making lists." Yep, I'm addicted to lists.

I'm definitely less stressed than the average person, and I have my lists to thank for that. Sure, there's still anxiety about getting everything crossed off a list, but I have tools and tricks for that. As a deadline-driven, Emmy Award–winning television producer in New York City, I owe a lot of my success to my lists. I've used them to get more done at work, to plan a destination wedding, and to find an apartment—just to name a few.

I've always been a list maker.

- ✓ Things to do
- ✓ Places to go
- ✓ Story ideas
- ✓ Apps to try
- ✓ Restaurants I love
- ✓ Books to read
- ✓ Events to plan

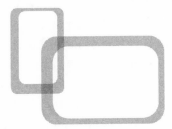

The lists go on and on. I even make lists of things to say in awkward situations, when buying a bra, and to make people smile. I've found that being as prepared as I can for every situation in life makes it much easier to be efficient. I realize not everyone is as compulsive about list making or research as I am, but I think you could be. That's why I wrote this book—to help you get your life back and not be overwhelmed.

OVERWHELMED MUCH?

I've always been afraid of change. When I was a kid, I hated getting a new teacher in grade school or moving to a new desk because I'd grown attached to what I knew. So when my husband, Jay, said he thought we should leave our home in Forest Hills in Queens and move to Manhattan, I did what I always do. I clammed up and rejected the idea. I thought, *Why do we need a new apartment? This one is fine!* Change is scary and unknown, and I have to work really hard at it.

Upper East Side, Midtown East, SoHo, Financial District, East Village, Gramercy—so many neighborhoods, and so little time. We checked every area we could find in Manhattan for a rental in our price range. But as soon as I got off the F train in Forest Hills and headed back to our apartment, I had already forgotten how many closets the apartment we looked at had, if it had an air conditioner, or what floor it was on! When you're renting, sometimes the listings aren't complete. They don't have pictures, and there are rarely floor plans. Normally, I'm very good at paying attention and staying focused, but for some reason, this assignment completely overwhelmed me. I was shocked, until I realized why.

LIFE IS EASIER WITH A LIST

I wasn't tackling this in a way that I knew from experience would work perfectly for me—with a list! After several disappointing and frustrating trips, I decided to make a checklist, just as I do at work. As a television and web producer in the Big Apple, I produce health segments in the studio and also in the field. That means I come up with story ideas, conduct interviews, book guests, prep anchors, time out segments, and much more. I realized that if I just applied some of the tools and techniques that have helped me to be successful at work, I would have no problem finding the perfect place.

When I produce segments, I use lists, checklists, and rundowns to keep myself better organized. So I made a checklist of all the things I needed to pay attention to when I was looking at an apartment: address, floor, view, hardwood floors or carpeting, number of closets, square footage, number of bedrooms and bathrooms, dishwasher, laundry, doorman, etc. This checklist became our rundown every time we stepped foot into an open house. Jay and I would refer to it as we walked through a space and ask questions accordingly. It allowed us to focus on exactly what we needed to pay attention to so that we could walk out with all the information we could possibly need to make a clear decision.

THINK LIKE A PRODUCER

Much like my shoot sheet at work, this roadmap helped me to pay attention and know exactly what I would come out with. If I'm going out on a field shoot to get elements for a video package, I always bring a list of all the questions I need to ask and the shots I need to get.

The day before a shoot, I sit at my desk and run through the entire interview in my head. I visualize exactly how it should go. For example, I'll interview the doctor first, then get exam video of the patient and doctor, and then interview the patient. I think about the purpose of the story and then write a list of all the questions to ask the doctor and the patient. This helps me make sure I don't leave anything out.

No matter how many shoots I've been on, I always do this extra prep work beforehand. Anything can happen, and distractions can be costly. In TV the last thing you want to do is return to the station without a critical shot. Sure, editors can work wonders, but without a shot of the doctor performing an important part of a procedure, your piece is dead.

Sometimes when I'm on a shoot, things don't go exactly as planned: a doctor has to step out during our interview to see a patient, or an emergency pops up. But with my checklist, I know exactly where we left off and what else needs to get done before I leave.

With my apartment checklists, I would go home and spread them all out in front of us so that Jay and I could compare listings. This helped us find a fabulous apartment in the East Village, where we loved living for four years.

LISTPRODUCER.COM

About a month after we moved, a friend started looking for an apartment. She told me how disorganized and overwhelmed she felt with her search and asked me for "that list you used." So I gave her my apartment-search checklist, and off she went. It helped her find the perfect apartment too. A real estate agent saw the checklist and asked her for a copy. He thought it was a great idea and wanted to share it with his clients so that they could stay focused and ask the right questions. My friend came back to me and said, "I think you're on to something with your lists."

In April 2011, I started ListProducer.com. It's a productivity site where I share my lists and other efficiency techniques, as well as ideas I've curated from experts in various areas. Listful thinking, as I call it, can be applied to anything in life and almost all situations. My intention with the site is to help people become more efficient, productive, and less stressed in all that they do.

LISTFUL THINKING

Here's what this book can do for you:

- ✓ Make you more productive and efficient both at work and at home
- ✓ Give you new strategies, and fix bad list-making habits
- ✓ Free up more time to do the things you really want to do

✓ Guide you to outsource aspects of your life so that you don't have to do everything all the time

✓ Introduce you to apps, services, and websites that can help you stay organized

✓ Help you give better gifts, throw better parties, and be more engaged because you'll have the time

✓ Be less stressed

SET INTENTIONS

This is a big one. Get ready to breathe a big sigh of relief. But first, you have a list-making assignment: make a list of the three things you hope to get out of this book. Your intention can be anything I just listed or something else, like "be more organized." It's up to you. I'll be guiding you from chapter to chapter to reach your goals list by list.

A LITTLE EXTRA HELP

I hope this book will help you spring into action and get more done. But I realize that sometimes it's tough to get motivated, so I'm going to give you a helping hand. I've designed a toolkit to evaluate where you could use more lists and how they can serve you best. There will be some goodies there to keep you focused and help you reach your goals. Download it all for free at ListProducer.com/ListfulThinkingGuide.

CHAPTER 1

What Can Lists Do for You?

What do Madonna, Martha Stewart, Richard Branson, John Lennon, Ellen DeGeneres, Ben Franklin, Ronald Reagan, Leonardo da Vinci, Thomas Edison, and Johnny Cash have in common? Each is or was a list maker. These successful people, along with many CEOs and busy entrepreneurs, all use lists to keep track of their ideas, thoughts, and tasks.

A recent survey from the career website LinkedIn.com found that 63 percent of all professionals frequently create to-do lists. Whether or not they use those lists correctly is another story. In fact, that same study found that only 11 percent of people who make lists said they accomplished everything on them in a given week. (http://linkd.in/1wIXxe8)

GET YOUR LIFE BACK

Time—it's one of those things we can never seem to get enough of. We are all trying to do a million things in our work, home, and social lives. Finding enough hours in the day to get everything done and still have downtime can be a struggle. It's no wonder so many of us are stressed, overextended, and exhausted.

More than half of all American employees feel overwhelmed, according to a study from the Families and Work Institute. The to-do lists go on and on. Just a single day can look like this:

✓ Complete a project at work

✓ Drive kids to dance class

✓ Clean out the garage

✓ Look for a new job

✓ Plan a vacation

✓ Meet friends for drinks

✓ Etc.

LISTFUL THINKING
. . . .

Many people say they wish they could be more successful, have more money, be happier, and feel healthier—yet they can't seem to achieve these things. They blame their bad luck, their busy lives, their limited resources, and so on. But our lives can actually be turned around with a simple piece of paper (or an app)—something so easy, anyone can do it.

Being more successful in any area of your life isn't about wishful thinking. It's about *listful thinking*. Aside from being a cute play on words, listful thinking works extremely well. Here's how. Once you write down a goal, you instantly become accountable. Whether that goal is to pick up eggs at the market or to write a book, the general intention is the same, to get what you want out of life (and to cross that item off your to-do list).

If you're part of the 54 percent who feel like they're chasing their own tail, I've got news for you: it doesn't have to be that way. You can still find time to relax, read a good book, and do the things you love. If you embrace the philosophy of listful thinking, you can get your life back—because thinking in terms of bite-sized goals is much easier than biting off a Guy Fieri–sized chunk.

Managing your to-dos, activity planning, problems, and almost any task you're faced with will be much easier with a list. I'll show you how to:

✓ Write lists that will help you get more done
✓ Save time

✓ Be more organized

✓ Be more productive

✓ Save money

✓ Reduce stress

✓ Be more successful at work and at home

BENEFITS OF LIST MAKING

Making lists will help you not only achieve your goals but also make you less stressed, more balanced, and less rushed. We've all been there: you discover you forgot your toothbrush after a long trip, or you go to the store but don't buy the black pants you went there to purchase in the first place. If you had written it down, you wouldn't have forgotten. (Okay, sometimes we *still* forget, but we are less likely to forget when we put it on paper.) Lists act as stress relievers, goal achievers, and life-savers. They will save you time and money because you'll be prepared for any situation.

List maker or not, everyone can benefit from this low-tech tool. Lists will turn even the most disorganized person into an organized thinker. It's all about preparation and thought-fulness.

Did You Know?
Famous List Makers

Madonna has been known to write up lists while cruising around in her limo, between shows, or while running errands. Her lists include things to do, stuff to buy, appointments, and contacts, and they have been auctioned for thousands of dollars. (http://bit.ly/1xke33k)

THE POWER OF LISTS

"You become what you believe" has been my mantra for some time—thanks to Oprah Winfrey. I was one of those people who watched her show religiously. When I was just thirteen years old, I was obsessed with *The Oprah Winfrey Show* and decided to write a letter to my hero. I got a response on official Oprah letterhead, along with an autographed photo. Check out the letter on the next page.

I love that the letter says "time does not permit me to answer all your questions." I can only imagine how many questions I had as an inquisitive "junior journalist"!

Anyway, "You become what you believe" is one of Oprah's most famous sayings, but she actually borrowed it from Maya Angelou. It's by far my favorite life lesson. It's true: if you believe it, you can become it!

OPRAH
THE OPRAH WINFREY SHOW

May 10, 1993

Dear Paula,

Thank you for taking the time to write to me. Although time does not permit me to answer all your questions, please know I enjoyed reading your letter and hope that you are working hard in school. Keep up your grades. Excellent grades are the key to great success.

Again, thanks for writing and watching The Oprah Winfrey Show.

Kind Regards,

Oprah Winfrey

OW/mm

Eight of My Favorite Oprah Quotes

Oprah Winfrey has taught me so much about giving, being a good listener, and striving to achieve my goals. She's been a part of my life since I began watching her show when I was young and has become more of a role model as I've gotten older.

1. "You become what you believe."

2. "When people show you who they are, believe them the first time."

3. "Turn your wounds into wisdom."

4. "You know you are on the road to success if you would do your job and not be paid for it."

5. "I trust that everything happens for a reason, even when we're not wise enough to see it."

6. "Surround yourself with only people who are going to lift you higher."

7. "When you know better—you do better."

8. "I don't believe in failure. It's not failure if you enjoyed the process."

Once you set an intention to do something, it is much easier to follow through. You become:

✓ Accountable

✓ Motivated

✓ Reminded more often of your intention

The act of writing something down is powerful. In fact, Dr. Gail Matthews, a professor at the Dominican University of California, found that writing down goals will make you 33 percent more likely to achieve them.

This rule applies to simple things like getting milk as well as more complicated tasks like finding a new job or having a difficult discussion with a loved one. Having a list makes you a better version of yourself, a more organized and determined version. Another nice thing is that the benefits are the same, no matter what the task is. Here are some of the benefits you can expect from list making.

1. List making will reduce anxiety. How many times have you said, "I have a million things to do. How am I going to get them all done?" A list will help to ease those fears. As soon as you start writing things down on paper (or in your smartphone) and get them out of your head, your stress levels will drop.

Plus we are forgetful. It's true: the average adult attention span is fifteen to twenty minutes, so we are bound to let a few tasks fall through the cracks. But we don't have to. As you think of something, write it down in a central place—the pad on your refrigerator door, a sticky note on your desk, in an e-mail, or even in your cell phone's calendar. I need to write down a task right as it comes into my head or else poof! I'm on to something else and it's gone. Taking just a few seconds to write down a task will save you so much time and aggravation later.

2. List making will boost your brain power. The act of making a list uses parts of your brain that might not normally get used. So you're working your brainpower and staying sharp while you organize your life. Memory expert Cynthia Green, PhD, wrote a guest post for my blog on how list making can save our brain. As she put it, "Memory tools, such as list making, force us to pay closer attention to the information we need to remember, and they give that information meaning by placing it in an organizational scheme."

3. List making will improve your focus. Using your list as a roadmap will allow you to keep your eye on the prize. Having a tool to sharpen your focus will help you in all aspects of your life. You'll find that soon you're getting much more done throughout the day and that you have time to do the things you really love.

Staying focused gets tougher and tougher by the day when you lead a busy life. Have you ever tried to write an e-mail to a client or a friend and then been sidetracked because another e-mail popped up? So you stop writing e-mail number one and start writing e-mail number two, when the boss calls or the kids cry or the delivery guy arrives...Aah! Get the picture?

A list makes it easy to refer back to what you were doing before you were interrupted. If you need to write John back, but your boss calls, write on your to-do list, "E-mail John." You know as well as I do that as soon as you hang up the phone, something else will grab your attention. Writing it down is so simple. It might seem silly, but it's incredibly effective.

Pop-Up Productivity Tip
Never Answer Your Phone Again!

Distractions are the worst. They will tank your productivity in no time. I have a little trick for you to make sure you stay productive throughout the day, and it is always, always, always to make an appointment with someone to have a phone conversation.

I never pick up the phone unless I know who it is and I'm scheduled to talk to that person at that time. I know it can seem mean and rude, but the second you pick up that phone, you're derailed. Right? You were in the middle of doing something else, and now you're talking to this person, with whom you may be working on a project. It may be important, but it's going to steer you away from your plan for the day. Now you're going to be doing things you didn't really intend to do right then, and the thing you were working on before the phone call is now ten steps behind you. This is why I always have people make appointments. Always. So if the phone rings and we don't have an appointment, I'm not answering.

Try it! It will help you get through the day—I promise.

4. List making will increase your self-esteem. One of my favorite things to do is crossing something off my list. Once you do this, you will feel an amazing sense of accomplishment too. Sometimes I even write down things I've done that weren't on my original list just so I can cross them off! This boost of self-esteem really helps to keep me motivated and productive. Knowing that you're able to get things done will also push you to do even more. Dr. Green, the memory expert, notes how lists help us to experience a sense of control. When we're an active participant in our lives, we feel much more empowered. Getting more done will help you feel more effective and capable too.

5. List making will organize your thoughts. Sometimes when I'm faced with a tough decision or even planning something like a vacation, I like to get all my thoughts down on paper. When I write a list and think about all the steps that will help me accomplish my goal, I feel much more prepared to tackle what's ahead. If you declutter your mind by writing out lists, your thoughts can be less jumbled.

6. List making will enable you to be prepared. The official motto of the Girl Scouts of America, "Be prepared," holds quite a bit of weight. Though I never was a Girl Scout, I hold this motto near and dear to my heart. I always have a snack, a piece of paper, and a pencil on hand. You just never know! The same goes for every event in life: we must be prepared. Whether we are looking for an apartment or job hunting, we need a list to keep our priorities in check.

THE DIFFERENCE BETWEEN A LIST AND A CHECKLIST

We often use the terms interchangeably, but lists and checklists are different animals. A list can be a to-do list, a pro-and-con list, or even a list of things you like about your spouse. But a checklist is something else. A checklist is a formula for getting something accomplished. All sorts of mistakes can be avoided with a simple checklist.

PICTURE IT: AN AVOIDABLE MISTAKE

My very first TV job was at WLNY-TV 55 on Long Island. (Random fact: It's also where I met my hubby.) One night at that station will live on in infamy—all because of a stupid and avoidable mistake.

That night the main anchor was on vacation, so one of the reporters was filling in for him on the 11:00 p.m. newscast. By day, we were interns and writers; by night, we were tape (yes there were still tapes then), teleprompter, and camera operators! That fateful night, the clock struck 11, and camera one's red light went on. We were live.

The fill-in anchor read the show's opening perfectly. She then turned to camera three, as scripted, for the next story— except that there was no script! Eeek! An anchor's nightmare: no teleprompter. The substitute anchor stumbled and looked down at her paper scripts. She scrambled to make it look as though nothing were wrong. But it was obvious to her, the viewers, and everyone involved in the production that something had gone awry.

That night, during our "postmortem" meeting—in which we discussed the good, the bad, and the ugly of the show—the substitute anchor threw the camera operator right under the bus. It wasn't pretty. Turns out, an intern (not me!) was on camera three that night and forgot to turn on the teleprompter. Boy—that did not go over well.

The next day there was an announcement from our news director: "Everyone must fill out a checklist before operating a studio camera!" As you can imagine, this idea was met with eye rolling and groaning. But we did it. Every one of us completed this form before every single show in the two years that I worked there:

✓ Turn on teleprompter.

✓ Set tilt.

✓ Set drag.

✓ Check focus.

✓ Check in on headset.

These are all simple things to do, but it's easy to get distracted and not do one of them. And as we all saw, that could be a disaster.

CHECKLIST MANIFESTO

Having a little extra help by way of a list can benefit people from all walks of life. It's been working for airline pilots and doctors for years. In *The Checklist Manifesto* by Atul Gawande, a surgeon at Brigham and Women's Hospital in Boston, he notes that airline pilots have preflight checklists as well as crisis checklists in case anything goes wrong in flight. It may seem unnecessary because the pilots are professionals who know what they're doing, but it's very easy to forget simple steps when you're under pressure. A checklist helps them to remember the simple stuff that might get overlooked.

FLYING 101

Thirteen is the magic number. That's roughly how many check-lists pilots will go through from the time they settle into the cockpit until they arrive at the destination. That's what Patrick Smith, a commercial airline pilot for over twenty years and author of *Cockpit Confidential*, told me. He said the actual checklists and what they're called vary from airline to airline, but all give guidelines for every leg of the trip, from before takeoff through the plane's final landing. "I can't imagine operating a flight without one. I mean, that's how engrained it becomes with us. I would feel naked without a checklist," says Smith.

Pilots are trained to remember some of these tasks, but there are times when they grab their *Quick Reference Handbook*, which is filled with lists for unlikely events. "That's a very fat book that contains literally hundreds of checklists, and those are used in situations that are not normal. There's something about functions. If there's some kind of emergency or system failure, you go to that book, and it leads you through theories of what you would probably better describe as a 'do' list," Smith says.

Although I don't take people's lives into my hands, I also use a checklist for every field shoot I go on. As I already mentioned, several days before a shoot, I go over the interviews in my head and write out the questions I want to ask. I've started every single interview I've ever conducted the exact same way: "Please say and spell your first and last name." Yet I still write a note that says "name/age/occupation" at the top of my question list. I don't want to have to remember to remember it. I also write out every shot I want to get while we're in the field. After doing this for years, it seems like such a simple task, but I never skip the step of making my checklist because if there were a surprise, I don't want to forget the easy stuff.

> **"Small doesn't mean unimportant."**
> —*Patrick Smith, airline pilot*

Dr. Gawande has worked with the World Health Organization to get checklists into hospitals around the world because of the benefits they've given pilots and high-rise construction workers. His team started with a nineteen-point checklist in 2008. Six months later, eight hospitals being studied saw a 36 percent drop in major postsurgical complications.

I asked Dr. Christopher Roseberry, a surgeon in New Hampshire specializing in minimally invasive procedures, about using checklists in the operating room. He e-mailed me back with this: "By having a simple checklist order sheet, pre-operative orders became easy, and our success at implementing the SCIP measures (Surgical Care Improvement Project, started in 2003 by the Centers for Disease Control) rose nearly 100 percent. In fact, the outliers were patients who somehow got to the operating room without having a set of pre-printed checklist orders on their chart. The checklist takes the fallible memory out of the equation."

See—checklists work!

LISTS AREN'T JUST FOR GROCERY SHOPPING

After starting my blog Listproducer.com in April 2011, I began hearing about lists being used in other ways, not just for making decisions and remembering groceries and to-dos. Lists can also be used for healing, health, achievement, and personal enrichment.

Post 9/11, Janice Holly Booth, author of *Only Pack What You Can Carry*, looked in the mirror and didn't like the person staring back. Like many of us who watched the worst terrorist attack in U.S. history unfold on our television screens, she began to reevaluate her life. "I knew I was a judgmental person. I wasn't hateful, but I was judgmental, and once you start judging, it leads you down that wrong road," she admits.

A CEO for a Girl Scout Council in North Carolina, Janice learned from her coworkers and friends that although she was a very kind person, at times she came off as harsh, rigid, and dismissive. Janice says she felt as if she were going insane and was deeply hurt because that wasn't how she saw herself.

Nonetheless, she was determined to make a change. "I did realize that the wound was deep and that I had to heal it. But I didn't know how. What I did know how to do was to make a list." Janice says that list saved her life. It wasn't a to-do list. It was a to-become list.

This is just one of many examples where making a list changed someone's life for the better. Lists can be used as roadmaps to do just about anything.

LIST MAKING AS THERAPY

There's a therapeutic and calming effect to writing a list. Getting the thought out of your head and into a central location allows us to be less stressed about having to remember something. If it's written down or stored in your phone, you don't have to remember to remember it.

Psychologists and psychiatrists often suggest that their patients make lists to avoid anxiety. Using lists to map out the pros and cons of a situation is also extremely helpful when making a difficult decision. "It takes mental work to keep things filed and stored and organized in your brain. And I think we underestimate how taxing it is to think," Atlanta-based psychiatrist and psychotherapist Tracey Marks points out. We all know the emotional and physical toll this type of mental stress can have on us, like lack of sleep, tense shoulders, and mood swings. Marks suggests that list making is like "opening a drain to let some of the build up just flow out."

Keeping stress in balance is crucial to our health and well-being. "The human system can't contain high levels of stress or

17

stimulation for long periods of time. It just can't," says Heidi Hanna, author of *Stressaholic: 5 Steps to Transform Your Relationship with Stress.* "Everything is supposed to have a rhythm and when we flatline like that, it can be deadly."

WE LOVE LISTS

As a society, we are fascinated with lists.

- ✓ David Letterman's Top Ten List
- ✓ Bestseller lists
- ✓ Lists of blockbuster movies
- ✓ List of richest celebrities (usually my girl Oprah makes it to the top)
- ✓ Lists of random facts
- ✓ Checklists for moving
- ✓ Lists of questions to ask your doctor

Did You Know?

David Letterman's very first top ten list debuted in 1985 and was the "Top Ten Words That Almost Rhyme with Peas."

You name it; we list it. There are websites and blogs (like my own, ListProducer.com) dedicated to lists of all sorts. Aside from their practical and predicable format, lists serve another important purpose. Checklists for any task will keep the reader focused, motivated, and organized, ensuring a successful outcome. "You know we are little creatures of habit. It's whatever we can do to make it easier for ourselves. I think people look at list making too as a sort of anal-retentive, type-A personality, but I'm like, no, for me it gives freedom," says Tracy McCubbin, a professional organizer and owner of dClutterfly.

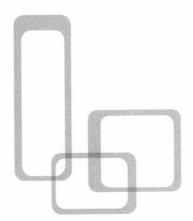

CHAPTER 2

Not All Lists Are Created Equal

The simplest purpose of a list is to aid you to remember what you need to do or to pick up at the grocery store. But more importantly, it should serve as a roadmap and a place from which to springboard your actions. I've already noted how much I love to-do lists because they keep me on track, but these are not the only kinds of lists you should be making.

THE GOOD, THE BAD, AND THE INDECISIVE: A PRO-AND-CON LIST

Any decision you ever make in life, for the most part, will have good and bad aspects.

- ✓ Buying a house
- ✓ Changing jobs
- ✓ Having a child
- ✓ Planning your honeymoon

All the events listed above involve big considerations and should be given critical thought. Enter: the pro-and-con list. It's best used when there isn't a clear yes or no answer to your question. I tend to weigh only two issues at a time; otherwise, I might end up even more confused than I was before.

"When you are forced to devise a list of pros and cons, it makes you dig deeper in thinking of all the possibilities—things that are easily overlooked if they're all in your head," says Tracey Marks, an Atlanta-based psychiatrist and psychotherapist. "It's easy to reduce it down to something like it's a great job because I get to work from home, but you've forgotten about the fact that you get health benefits or this, that, and the other."

Here's how to effectively make a pro-and-con list that will reduce stress and move you closer to an answer more quickly.

1. Paper or digital? I'm a paper-and-pencil kind of girl, but I also love using apps and technology for list making. I find that if I like the paper I'm writing on, then I'm more likely to sit down and make a pro-and-con list even for a really difficult decision. I've also made several on a fun pre-made pro-and-con list from KnockKnockStuff.com. But you can also use plain paper and crease it down the middle to list your own pros and cons. The results are the same. Ditto for digital lists.

2. Start listing. Whenever I make a pro-and-con list for the first time with an issue, I write down whatever comes to mind—even if it seems like a minor detail, such as the office of a potential job is painted green and that's your favorite color. Put it in the pro column. You can weed things out later. List as few or as many pros and cons as you like.

Think like a journalist when you do this part of the process. In my very first journalism class, in high school, we were taught "the five Ws":

1. Who?
2. What?
3. Where?
4. When?
5. Why?

Think of these details when you begin your list. You need to be objective and to look at the facts first. Try not to inject too much opinion while you make this list. Just get everything down on paper. You can prioritize and give each item weight later.

3. Revise. Once you've written down all your thoughts, assign value to them. Does the fact that the apartment you're looking to buy is on a two-way street bother you? If so, that factor goes on the con list. Go back through the thoughts you've listed and delete those that either don't matter or won't affect your decision. If the green office isn't swaying your thought process either way, then cross it out. Use this process to make your list helpful. Also, consolidate similar points so that you don't end up with a long list that could overwhelm you.

4. Sleep on it. After you've made a final list, put it away and rest your brain. It can be hard to think straight if you've been staring at something for a long time. Come back to your list tomorrow. When you return, you might look at your pro-and-con list in a totally different light.

5. Weigh your options. This doesn't mean that just because you have five items in the pro column and only three in the con column, that the pros have won. Think about each option critically and envision what your life would be like if you had to deal with each one. Do some research if you need to, or ask some questions. Remember that what might not seem like a big deal to someone else, may be to you. Be realistic, and be true to yourself.

If you're having trouble, try the website Proconlists.com. What you can do there is input all the pros and cons that are floating around in your head and then assign them weight, depending on how rational an item is and how emotional it is for you. An algorithm on the website figures out what you should do after you've entered all your items. I don't think you should necessarily use this website as the deciding factor, but it can be a good exercise for evaluating each item more closely.

6. Talk it out. If you're having difficulty deciding what to do, talk with a friend, your spouse, or a coworker. Two minds are better than one. This person might even point out benefits and disadvantages that you haven't yet considered.

THE ART OF THE PACKING LIST

There are two essential reasons to make a packing list before every trip:

1. You'll inevitably forget something you need without one.
2. You'll save money if you have one.

Those are two pretty big reasons. Showing up to a remote tropical island without your bathing suit is a big bummer. Sure, there is probably a gift shop at the resort where you can buy an overpriced bathing suit, but why would you want to do that? It's a waste of your money and your time.

Speaking of money, according to the Bureau of Transportation Statistics, the largest American airline carriers made $3.5 billion dollars in baggage fees in 2012. Yep, that's billion with a B. All those $25 dollar fees per bag add up quickly. Let's say you and your family go on vacation at least once a year, and there are three of you. That's $25 times three, which equals

$75. That's $75 spent before you start having any fun on your vacation. What could you do with an extra $75? I'm thinking hair blowouts, mani-pedis, or new shoes for starters.

What does this have to do with a packing list? Well, being organized and prepared for any trip means you'll bring fewer "just-in-case items" and bring only what you really need. As a result, you pack less and save money. It's an easy concept but not so easy to apply. I admit it takes a bit of pre-planning and some discipline. But once you try it, you will be hooked. Here is my strategy: I make a brand new packing list for every trip. Some people keep a template of items they use often, but I like to start from scratch to customize my list. Having the list helps to make my trip less stressful.

1. Write an itinerary. Let's say I'm going to the beach from Friday to Monday. I write down all the days that I'll be staying and all of the activities I'll be doing so that I can get an idea of what kind of clothes to bring:

Friday: travel, dinner, sleep

Saturday: beach, dinner, sleep

Sunday: beach, boat excursion, dinner, sleep

Monday: travel

Don't think only in terms of clothes but also of other items you might need. If you're museum hopping, for example, you won't want to forget your camera or your comfy shoes.

2. Make categories. Now that you have an idea of what you'll be doing each day, identify categories for each of the items you'll need. I break up my packing list into sections:

✓ Toiletries

✓ Clothes and Shoes

✓ Jewelry

✓ Electronics and Books

✓ Travel Needs (Like Documents)

✓ Last-Minute Items

A list of categories makes it easier to consider more items. It's easy to get overwhelmed when you take on the task of a list that simply begins "pack," but it's not so overwhelming when you break it down into bite-sized pieces.

3. Review your daily routine. I run through my morning in my head to make sure I don't leave anything behind when I'm traveling, such as dental floss or deodorant. This will also help you avoid getting to your destination without your toothbrush!

4. Check the weather. The weather forecast is not always 100 percent accurate, but at least the forecast gives me a sense of what types of things I might need, such as a hat, sunscreen, or maybe an umbrella. Another good trick is to lean on technology to inform you about the weather.

Pop-Up Productivity Tip

I'm in love with the app "Dark Sky." It tracks where you are and gives you a heads up when it's about to rain. You get a friendly little message that some precipitation is headed your way in, say, fifteen minutes and that it will last for about six minutes. It's that precise. (You will find more apps to make your life easier in Chapter 8.)

5. Pick outfits. I find that picking actual outfits instead of just throwing some clothes into my bag keeps me from over-packing. Go through your closet and pull out the combinations you want to wear, including the shoes and the jewelry. I always pack a pashmina in my carry-on because it can double as a blanket on the plane.

Tracy McCubbin, the professional organizer and owner of dClutterfly I mentioned earlier, does the same thing before she goes on any trip. "I've been traveling so much the last two years I was like 'I gotta deal with this because the anxiety before I fly is really bad.' So now I make a list of my outfits…I pack those, and it's done, and I get there. For me, list making of my outfits was a huge game changer," she says.

6. Make a last-minute list. This list is everything I'll need to use the morning I leave and can't pack until then. This list also includes tasks that need to be finished before I head out the door.

Anytime we went on vacation when I was a kid, which was

usually to Lake George, New York, my dad would list all the things that needed to be done before we left. The list consisted of things like turn off the air conditioning, put mail on hold, water plants, etc. He did this so that he wouldn't have to remember to remember anything. With a list, it's all right there, making the doing of the tasks quick and easy. It was a good lesson for me and probably explains why I'm such a list maker today.

TAKING A LONG TRIP?

Fear not! I have a solution. It is possible to travel for two weeks in Europe (or anywhere else) with only carry-on luggage. Nicole Feldman, my close friend and fellow Hofstra University alumna, has done it! It's true. She is a packing genius. Here are a few of her basic packing rules:

1. Roll everything.

2. Wear your heaviest items on the plane.

3. Get a light twenty-two-inch suitcase that rolls in any direction. This is the big investment that will save you so much time, money, and angst along the way. It's also the largest size suitcase that can be stored overhead, according to airline regulations.

4. Use a cute, light, and spacious purse as your shoulder bag, which will double as a travel tote during your sightseeing days.

5. Space Bags® are a must. These clear and easily flattened packing bags are available at Bed, Bath & Beyond. After

packing one of these bags, lay it flat on the ground, roll it from one end to the other, and watch as all of the air is compressed out of the bag. With the air compressed out of the bag, it becomes a much smaller bag. Two extra, empty Space Bags® can easily be slipped into the front pocket of a suitcase, and they're good to have on hand for dirty clothes on the way home.

Nicole shares her complete list on my blog, ListProducer.com. Take a look. It's a useful reference for any trip.

GET MOVING

The same attention should be paid if you're moving. No matter how much help you get from friends, family, or a moving company, relocating is stressful. Lists are your friends!

1. Downsize. Moving is the perfect time to reevaluate whether you need that third set of sheets you never use. List all the things you'd like to get rid of or donate.

2. Pack. Packing for a move is pretty easy. For the most part, you're taking everything, right? But it helps to label each box with the room it belongs to and a number, and then to make a list of every single item in each box according to its number. When you arrive at your new home, feeling overwhelmed, you'll soon know where everything you need on that first night is located. This is also a great trick if you're putting some items into storage.

3. Replace. One of the fun parts of moving is replacing things that you leave behind or sprucing up others. Make this list before you leave your old space; that way you have a framework set before you get to your new location. Some things, like furniture, will need to be planned out ahead of time.

4. Find new hangouts. This is another great perk of moving. A new neighborhood means new restaurants, stores, and entertainment choices. Start a list of all the spots you want to check out or research when you move. Asking new neighbors for their list of recommendations is also a great way to make new friends.

RESEARCH LISTS

The idea behind a research list is that you can work out the details for just about anything you need help planning:

- ✓ Places to get your hair cut in your new neighborhood
- ✓ Finding a housekeeper
- ✓ Learning to eat better
- ✓ Finding a home
- ✓ Planning a wedding
- ✓ Taking a trip
- ✓ Ways to make more money

Begin by making a list of all the things you hope to accomplish or to learn about your given topic. I often use this type of list when planning a trip or a big event. Everything can be broken down into lists to help you organize your thoughts.

Pop-Up Productivity Tip

If you're not a natural-born researcher, you may want to outsource the task. Outsourcing is an incredible way to save time and concentrate on the things you really want to be doing. (For resources on outsourcing, refer to Chapter 7.)

CATALOG LIST

When I said I make a list for everything, I wasn't kidding:

- ✓ Books to read
- ✓ Restaurants to try
- ✓ Mascaras I like
- ✓ Clothes I need to buy
- ✓ TV series to catch up on
- ✓ Gifts I'd like people to buy for me (seriously, this is a thing)
- ✓ Websites I want to visit

I like to call these lists catalog lists. These are lists of things, not tasks.

What do you do when someone tells you about a book you'll love? If you're like me, you want to remember the title but quickly get sidetracked, and poof! It's gone. It's not really our fault. Our memory dulls when we don't exercise it. I blame technology. Sure, a few phone numbers may be ingrained in our memory, but because of technology, we've stopped using this part of our brain. I haven't been able to remember my work cell phone number in seven years. I never committed it to memory because I don't have to. I admit: I sound pretty ridiculous when I leave messages asking people to call me back at "Um, uh, that number is...let me just get it for you here... Oh! There it is." If I had to remember it, I would, but the point is that I don't need to.

So the catalog list helps us when we need to keep track of similar information. Where you keep it, is up to you—but if you don't know where that list lives, then you've done yourself a disservice.

I rely on my smartphone and several apps to hold all my catalog lists. I'll be talking more about which apps help me the most in Chapter 8, "Let's Get Digital."

LIFE LIST

This is one of my favorite types of lists because it's so personal. If you aren't a list maker yet, start with a life list. A bucket list itemizes all the things you want to do before you "kick the bucket."

Did You Know?

According to Slate.com, the term "kick the bucket" has been around since at least 1785. A bucket list, though, is a newer addition to our vernacular. It became pretty popular in 2007 because of Jack Nicholson and Morgan Freeman's movie *The Bucket List,* in which two terminally ill men take a road trip together to cross off the items on their lists of what to experience before they die. (http://slate.me/1subN5t)

You know yourself better than anyone, so it's a fun list to put together. Do you want to learn to speak French, perform on Broadway, ride a cable car in San Francisco, or hold a koala bear in Australia? Any dream, however big or small, should go on this list.

I like to write my life list in a notebook, but you can do anything that works for you. MyLifeList.org is a great place to keep your list and to take a peek at others' lists. This website creates a community around achieving these goals. You can find people who have similar goals and discover what they're doing to make them come to fruition.

The value of a life list is immense. Yes, it's great to dream, but I believe that once you write something down, you set an intention that moves things in that direction—whether consciously or subconsciously.

NEW YEAR DIARY
• •

I chatted with list maker, businesswoman, world traveler, and author Melanie Young about her annual ritual of creating a New Year Diary. It includes all the places she wants to travel and what she wants to do that year.

Melanie's birthday is on January 1. After a very bad date one New Year's Eve, she resolved never to have a bad birthday again. From then on, she decided she would travel on her big day. "In each entry is a list. The first list is a summary of what happened that year: the highs and the lows. Then there is list of resolutions and what I want to have happen: twelve to fifteen resolutions. And I have done that since 1988," Melanie told me.

Melanie's lists have led to trips to Bangkok, Ho Chi Minh City, Machu Picchu, Rio, Belize, Honduras, Spain, France, and Hawaii—to name a few. She keeps these diaries lined up on a shelf and believes they may one day be her autobiography.

ASK, BELIEVE, RECEIVE
• •

I love the principles in the book *The Secret*. Quite simply, they get me a seat on a crowded New York City subway every day—and if you've ever been to New York, you know this is a small miracle. But I've also applied the principles to bigger things, such as going to *The Oprah Winfrey Show!* I think believing that I was going to get the tickets and visualizing myself in the audience helped too. My husband thinks this is all nonsense, but I've proven him wrong.

What is *The Secret*? The idea behind *The Secret* is that if you put something out into the universe, you are likely to receive it if you really believe in it. Since I was a little girl and before *The Secret* existed, my mother would always say to me, "Put it out there. You never know what will happen."

It's like when you talk about wanting a new job to everyone you know, and eventually, someone comes to you with a sweet opportunity. Sure, it could be coincidence, but I think putting it out there helps.

VISUALIZE YOUR GOALS

I'm not arts-and-crafty, but at the beginning of every year, I make a vision board. It's my one craft project for the year, and it's so much fun. Reading magazines is my guilty pleasure, and it comes in handy for this task. I rip out pages of pictures and words that speak to me, and then I glue my favorites onto a poster board.

WHAT IS A VISION BOARD?

A vision board is a place for all the things you'd like to accomplish, places you'd like to go, and things you enjoy. If you use this tool as a jumping off point for your goals, you are more likely to achieve them. I use it as a reminder of my goals, like having a three-bedroom apartment or going to Venice. I also put photos of people I admire, things I enjoy such as drinking tea, and other ambitions, including writing this book. It's imperative to be able to visualize your goals, even if only on paper. This all goes back to the credo, "You become what you believe."

THERE ARE NO RULES

Your vision board can include photos, drawings, or inspirational words. If you are super crafty, you can use fabric and other textures as well. There is no right way to do it. The photos can be places you've been, places you want to go, outfits you like, things you'd like to buy, kitchens you want to model yours after, or anything else that makes you smile.

You can be literal or creative with your choices. I've included photos of champagne because it's one of my favorite drinks, but also, it symbolizes celebrations. I'd like to have a lot of things to celebrate. Along that line, my vision board includes a photo of someone filling out thank-you cards, not because I particularly like writing thank-you cards but because I'd like to have lots of reasons to say thank you.

I purposely leave some white space on my vision board so that it can evolve throughout the year. Whenever I see a photo that catches my eye or I think of something I want to achieve, I add it. My vision board hangs inside my closet door. This way I'm sure to see it every morning when I get dressed. You can make your board by hand, the way I do, or you can make one digitally on your computer. Here are some places where you can keep your vision board:

1. On your desk in a frame
2. Pinned up on a cork board

3. As your desktop wallpaper

4. In a book that you carry with you

5. On your phone in an app, such as Vision Board Deluxe by Happy Tapper

6. On Pinterest.com

7. On Dreamitlive.com

I think this would be a fun activity to do with friends or even with kids. Kids can make their own vision boards with activities and places they want to go throughout the year. You'll be surprised how much of an influence these vision boards can have on them. You can even make it a tradition to check out last year's vision board on New Year's Eve to see how much they've done in the past year. Then make a new board on New Year's Day. But you don't have to do this at the beginning of the year; you can make a vision board at any time!

Remember, though, that just having a vision board isn't enough. We must actively work toward our goals.

GRATITUDE LIST

Sometimes I get in a funk—although for the most part, I'm a positive person. But sometimes I get down. It happens to the best of us. My remedy for these times is a gratitude list.

A gratitude list notes everything that you are happy about. It could include anything that makes you feel grateful:

✓ Mangos are in season.

✓ My favorite show is on tonight.

✓ The soufflé I made didn't deflate.

✓ My best friend moved into my neighborhood.

✓ I didn't burn myself making pizza.

✓ I got a promotion at work.

✓ My husband brought me a cute gift just because.

✓ I get to go on a trip to New Zealand.

The idea is to put anything that makes you smile on this list. Silly or serious—just write it down. This list can change your state of mind by reminding you of what really matters in your life. I think it was Oprah who said that people get too wrapped up in their everyday tasks and don't take the few minutes they should to reflect on what is really good about life.

My mom tries to find the positive in any situation, so I guess that's where I get this from. Some psychologists suggest making a gratitude list everyday for the benefits to be really effective. "I have a nightly practice in which I list the things that I'm grateful for. That's my personal gratitude practice…scientific studies have actually shown that being grateful increases your level of happiness," points out Alexis Sclamberg, self-help author and co-founder of Elevate Gen Y.

Aside from making you smile while you noodle about all the things you love in life, this practice can have some long-term benefits as well. "Having to unearth or discover these things that you weren't really appreciating makes you feel more gracious and thankful and can actually boost your self-esteem or your sense of self-worth," says psychotherapist Tracey Marks.

We all want to be happier right? So why not give the gratitude list a try.

CHAPTER 3

List Making 101

Whether you write a to-do list, a grocery list, or a list of pros and cons, the act of putting your thoughts down on paper will be good for your mind, body, and soul. I'm not kidding. Making a list will decrease stress, increase productivity, keep you organized and focused, and give you a sense of accomplishment.

"So there's that motivation of like, 'I'm getting things done!' And you're seeing that there's progress being made. Even if it's little things…it becomes momentum to push us forward," says Heidi Hanna, who wrote *Stressaholic: 5 Steps to Transform Your Relationship with Stress.*

Investing some time into this simple task offers big returns. My beloved journalism professor Cathy Krein always told us to "Keep it simple, stupid" when critiquing our writing. She meant that in the most loving way, and I think that statement can be applied to everything in life, including lists.

HOW TO MAKE THE ULTIMATE TO-DO LIST

It's easy to be overwhelmed by your list and ignore it. But I want to tell you how to make the ultimate to-do list and stick to it, and I can do that with a list.

1. Just write it down. It's easy to forget things that you don't have right in front of you, so write down any task you need to do as soon as you think of it. It doesn't matter if the list is in any particular order right now; just write it down.

2. Organize your list. Once you know many of the things you have to do, organize this list. Break it up into categories: work, home, kids, play, etc. Each area of your life should have its own list. Without categories, your list will overwhelm you, and then you will ignore them.

For the most part, I keep separate lists for separate things. So the work list is in my desk drawer at work, and the home list is on my desk drawer at home. I always know where these lists are and what types of things I'll find on them. It helps my mind compartmentalize. That way, when I look at the items on my list, I'm ready to tackle that type of task. You'd be surprised how helpful this can be.

"It keeps things in perspective, and it keeps you from getting overwhelmed with just too many things," Dr. Tracey Marks points out. She also suggests chunking out your day into times where you start and stop tasks you tend to get lost in, like checking your e-mail. Sticking to this kind of plan can streamline your attention, making you more efficient and productive.

3. Prioritize. Once you have your separate lists, go over the items on each and order them by deadline or importance. This will help you to stay on track and focus only on what needs to be done right now. While there may be other tasks that are easier to do, they might not be as important. Resist any temptation to jump into those tasks first just because they are easy; doing them will just put you behind schedule.

4. Rewrite. Now that you've organized your lists by category and determined what's most important, rewrite your list. By making a clean list, which is easy to read, you will be more likely to refer to it and check things off in order. I've been known to write and rewrite lists again and again. Find a system that works for you. I don't like a lot of clutter on my lists, so if a list is too messy, with all my notes everywhere, I will simply start over.

5. Repeat. In order to get things accomplished, make as many lists as you need to make. I make a list everyday and then add to it throughout the day. The next day I add the things that I didn't get to the day before, and so on.

BE A BETTER LIST MAKER

· ·

Yes, there is a correct and an incorrect way to make a list. Just putting things down on paper isn't enough. Having a laundry list of to-dos can make you feel anxious and overwhelmed, and the purpose of a list is to make you feel better, not worse.

"What I discovered is when I listed everything, it actually had this effect of paralyzing me. Because I could never possibly do all that," says Margaret Moore, who coauthored *Organize Your Mind, Organize Your Life*. She suggests working in "optimal doses." These are going to be different for everyone because only we know how we work best. "You've got to find this right dose where you feel organized and on top of things, and you don't feel overwhelmed. And it's a personal trial-and-error thing until you get that right," she explains.

Wherever you decide to write your list, there is always the issue of actually doing the things you've set out to accomplish. Once you've written a list, here are some easy ways to tame it.

1. Evaluate Your List.
Prioritize. I wrote about this before, and this could be the single most important factor when managing a to-do list. The truth is that maybe all of those items don't belong on your list after all. What really needs to get done now? And what can you save for another time?

Be realistic. This is always a tough one. You know yourself; you know what you're capable of doing. But sometimes it's difficult to be honest and realistic when it comes to a to-do list. I get it. You want to cross everything off now! But the ability to evaluate what makes sense to tackle first is valuable, and it will help tremendously. If you know that cleaning out your closet will take two hours and you have a doctor's appointment in a half hour, then it's not the best task to take on for the moment.

Focus. Making a pointed and specific list will help you streamline all your to-dos. Instead of writing "organize the garage," focus on the steps in your tasks. Writing out the steps to "organization" will help you get it done. Have your list note specific tasks, such as:

- ✓ Get rid of extra holiday decorations
- ✓ Organize the tools in one spot
- ✓ Clear clutter where the car should be parked

Using specific action words will keep you on target as well. Instead of writing "go to grocery store," put down "pick up salad, tomatoes, and avocados." This is a clearer direction. It will help to streamline your shopping and get you out of the store faster.

2. Consolidate Your List.
Small wins. Sometimes it's better to downsize. Putting a few easier tasks on your list can make you feel better because you're able to get them done quickly. I know I said earlier that you shouldn't just do the easiest tasks first—but sometimes, completing easier tasks will help with motivation. Do what you have to do to get and keep going.

Make different lists. Keeping everything you've ever wanted to accomplish in every area of your life on one list is a huge mistake. Make a different list for each project you work on so that you don't feel overwhelmed or confuse tasks.

3. Delegate Your List.

Outsource your list. A very wise woman—Leah Busque, CEO of TaskRabbit—once told me that just because you can do something doesn't mean you should do it. As a former control freak, I take these words to heart. (Okay, I'm still sort of a control freak, but not as much as I used to be.) Being able to delegate tasks instead of taking them on yourself will change your life. (We'll look at this more in Chapter 7, "Outsourcing Your Life Will Set You Free.")

Just say no. Wow! Imagine the things you could get done if you would pass on projects you really don't want to do. Yep, that one word, "no," will give you your life back. It's easy to agree to a coffee break or to see that movie your friend has been obsessed with for weeks, but it's important not to make "yes" your default answer. Remember that your time is valuable. So, it's okay not to volunteer to be a chaperone for that school trip or not to take on another project at work.

Don't get roped into joining something unless it's something you want to spend your time on. That way, you can create more free time in your schedule and stay more productive. This is easier said than done, but once you begin to do it, you'll be so much more productive.

I say no a lot, but I've learned to do so by practicing. For instance, I have Wednesdays after work all to myself. My husband usually works those nights, so I schedule dinners with girlfriends, or mani-pedis, and other fun stuff. Often, I use the time just for me. Sometimes when people ask us to do something and we have plans with our self, we are inclined to break them because we think, *Oh, I'm not doing anything anyway.* I've stopped thinking this way, and I'm much happier for it. I now value my need to catch up on some reading, or to relax and watch an episode of *Giada at Home,* or to work on my blog. The reason I don't break these plans is because they feed me. They make me happy because I really want to do them. They are just as important as going out with friends and any of the other social activities I might have.

Then comes the issue of work. Eeek! Sometimes it's really hard to say no there. Often we have no choice but to say yes. When that happens, I look at what else I have on my to-do list and offset something. For example, I'll ask someone else to jump in to help me finish one of the tasks or I'll give it to another team member.

Here are a few nice ways to say no:

- ✓ "I won't be able to do this project (or go to this event), but X would be a wonderful addition." (People love to be given solutions, plus you'll feel you did your part by finding a replacement.)

- ✓ "Please check back in with me in X weeks. My schedule will clear up then, and I'd love to help." (Be realistic about the holes in your calendar, and make sure to give yourself enough time.)

- ✓ "Normally I'd say yes right away, but I'm trying something new where I evaluate how much I take on.

Unfortunately, my plate is full right now, so I'll have to decline." (You'll be surprised how nicely people will respond to honesty and transparency.)

4. Set Deadlines.

As a TV producer, I know this step all too well. It really works. Giving yourself a deadline helps to cut down on unfinished tasks. If you trick your brain into believing that you need to create your Thanksgiving menu by Halloween, then you will do it. I start my holiday shopping in August every year for this exact reason. If I start early, I won't be as crazy when turkey day rolls around.

This approach works for simple to-dos as well. I often give time values to the items on my list. I know it will take me fifteen minutes to walk to the dry cleaners so I tell myself it needs to be done before 2:00 p.m. This way I work it into my schedule and ensure it gets done.

Pomodoro Technique

There's a time-management approach called the Pomo-doro technique that might help. Francesco Cirillo developed it in the 1980s and is named after a tomato-shaped kitchen timer. The idea is that you divide tasks into "pomo-dori" (Italian for tomatoes) of twenty-five minute intervals. Then you can take a break after you reach that twenty-five minute mark.

I like this idea because twenty-five minutes is much more manageable than say a full hour. Sometimes we think "I'll devote an hour to this task," but think about how much time you actually spend getting distracted during that hour. This way you are focused for a short amount of time and more likely to succeed.

I use a similar technique where I look at the clock and make deals with myself. So let's say it's 12:36 p.m. and I really need to research a gift for my mom's birthday. I will say to myself "I can focus on this task until 1:00 p.m. and then go on to something else." So in that specific time frame, I'm only focused on that one task. I know when it will end and that there is a deadline so I'm more likely to do it.

5. Reward Yourself

Oh! This is my favorite step. Bribery goes a long way when it comes to a to-do list. Giving yourself something to look forward to will make crossing off your to-dos even more enticing. I make deals with myself constantly—for example, *If I finish writing this script then I can spend ten minutes on Facebook.* You'll be surprised how eager you'll be to get everything crossed off your to-do list as a result.

6. Remind Yourself.

We can't all remember every single thing we need to do. It's impossible. So, go easy on yourself and set reminders. It's easy to ignore your to-do list and never check off the tasks on it. But if you set reminders, you will remember to look at the list. I do this several times throughout the day by sending meeting makers in Outlook to myself on things I need to remember to do. In addition to my handwritten list, these pop-up reminders help me to get everything done on deadline.

LOCATION, LOCATION, LOCATION

Where should you write this list? Wherever you're going to actually use it. Where you make your lists is just as important as why you make them.

GOOD THINGS COME IN SMALL PACKAGES

For some people, keeping a list the size of a sticky note is their answer. With a limited number of hours in the day, there is only so much that can be accomplished. So it makes sense to set ourselves up for success.

✓ Tracy McCubbin, the professional organizer and owner of dClutterfly I mentioned earlier, uses sticky notes in addition to a longer list she carries so that she can cover all her bases. "I have what I call my master list, which lives on a legal pad, and then I have a Post-it® on top of it that is filled with the things that are actionable within the next couple of days. So I'll aggregate the things that need to get done faster," she explains.

It's much easier to get three things done than it is to get thirty things done. That's just simple math! Tracy's method can be used to increase productivity at work, to plan social events, and even to limit overspending at the grocery store. Not convinced? Here's a list of reasons to limit your to-do list to fit on a sticky note:

1. The limited space of a sticky note (the squares are only 3" x 3") will force you to prioritize quickly. You list the most important tasks first, lest you run out of precious yellow space!

2. When you've completed everything on the tiny list, you're done for the day! You can use you free time to—dare I say it—relax!

3. Life happens, and when it does, you will be glad that "organize your sock drawer" and "subscribe to ListProducer.com" are the only tasks left on your list.

4. They stick! Depending on my tasks for the day, I've been known to stick my list on the corner of my laptop, the back of my cell phone, and even my bathroom mirror. Sometimes something as simple as keeping your to-do list in a place where you're sure to see it will increase your productivity.

5. A full sticky note prevents you from adding tasks throughout the day. Sometimes I feel like I will never complete all the items on my list, only to realize my list has doubled in size throughout the day.

Did You Know?
Six Facts You Probably Didn't Know about the Post-it® Note

They are everywhere—colorful squares, tiny translucent flags. Wherever you are, you're likely near a Post-it®. People everywhere depend on them for reminders, to-do lists, and staying organized. At any one time I may have a flurry of sticky notes on my desk, on loose pieces of paper, folders, magazine pages, and even on my phone!

But did you ever stop to think about how those sticky little squares came to be? Check out these facts you never knew about the Post-it® note:

1. The tiny reminders were actually created in 1968 by accident. (Nope, Romy and Michele didn't invent them after all.)

2. Spencer Silver, a 3M scientist, created the reusable adhesive in 1968 while trying to make a super strong adhesive.

3. 3M developer Arthur Fry used the adhesive on his bookmark inside his songbook at church. He eventually developed the idea with 3M's blessing.

4. The original canary yellow color of the note was also an accident. It just so happened to be the color of the scrap paper used to test the adhesive.

5. Post-it® notes hit the stores in 1980.

6. Canary yellow notes remain the biggest seller, even though a variety of colors are available.

GO BIG OR GO HOME

Notebooks are my list paper of choice—for the most part. I like the lines and the extra space to write as much as I want. I have a bunch of big notebooks for different projects and tasks. For instance, I've kept one for writing this book. A purple one-subject notebook is filled with questions to ask during interviews, outlines of chapters, and to-dos with deadlines. At work, I have a spiral steno pad that is bound on the top, because I'm a lefty and sometimes the spirals poke at me.

I love sticky notes as much as the next organizing geek, but sometimes they aren't the best place for a massive mind dump. And though they're small and sticky, they can still be lost. (I'll get into what to do if you constantly lose your lists in Chapter 8, which is my love letter to all things digital.) As big a fan of digital list-making tools as I am, there's something about handwriting your lists. I think we're better able to connect with handwritten lists for some reason.

"There is a difference between having something on a piece of paper that you can easily grab versus an app that you've got to log into or turn your phone on…that's a lot of steps to get to the information you need versus 'here it is; I can hold it; I can turn it around; I can touch it; I can put it in a drawer,' " Dr. Tracey Marks points out.

My handwriting has become progressively worse over the years because I type and text more than I write. But I make it a point to write out my daily to-do lists at work in pencil in a notebook. In an article titled "Is Handwriting Becoming Extinct?" in the August 2013 issue of *Martha Stewart Living*, writer Joanne Chen cites a study from Indiana University.

Researchers tested two groups of preschoolers with MRIs. One group learned their letters and symbols by typing them, the other group learned by writing them. The kids who typed couldn't see the difference between letters and shapes, while the kids who wrote by hand could. What this shows is that writing things by hand does help our brain to learn and remember better than we do if we only type.

I think passwords are a perfect example of this. I constantly forget my passwords, and it's irritating. Because I'm always mindlessly typing them, they get lost in my brain. If I physically wrote them all down, I know I would better remember them.

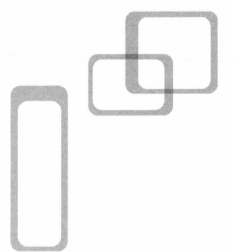

CHAPTER 4

Work It: Lists at Work Make You More Successful

One of the ongoing themes I've learned from maintaining a blog about lists is that successful people use them everyday. CEOs, managers, and directors in all industries use them. It doesn't matter what you do for a living, a list will help you do it better.

ORGANIZE YOUR DAY WITH A LIST

The most important thing to remember when becoming a list maker or learning how to do it better is that you have to find a technique that works best for you. Not all the solutions I give will fit you; you must customize your list making to serve you best.

I use my to-do list as my "master command center"

throughout the day. It's filled with tasks, notes, reminders, and more. But everything is very segmented, so I don't confuse myself. Don't worry; I'll explain.

I recently got an e-mail from Josh, who reads my blog at ListProducer.com. He wrote: "I do enjoy making lists and find them helpful. However, one thing that I get stuck with is how to set up my list. I often find that I get stumped with this step. I want my lists to look presentable and not just write stuff any and everywhere. How do you set yours up?"

Great question! At work, I write a list every night before I leave my desk. No matter what time it is or if I'm running late for an appointment, I make my list. Sometimes I start writing this list during the day, as I think of things. But I always write it the day before because I like to come to work and hit the ground running in the morning. With my list, I have a roadmap in front of me showing me where my day will go. It helps me to feel less stressed first thing in the morning and to get started on what needs to get done first.

I detail every single thing that needs to happen the next day on my work list that is kept on my steno pad. Each day has its own page with a to-do list. Here's my process:

1. Write the date at the top. This helps when you need to look back for information later.

2. Detail every single thing that has to happen the next day, including the stuff you do every day. Trust me: distractions happen, so you may need this extra reminder. Plus it's just more fun to be able to cross off things you know you'll do.

3. Prioritize by deadline. I like to write my list in the order that things need to happen. I will write "11:00 a.m." to the left of my note about a phone appointment I've set up for that time. This helps me stay focused throughout the day.

Great! Now that your own list is made, you are all set, right? Nope. Other stuff will pop up. I promise. So you need to be flexible and add to your list as needed. Here's what I do:

1. Add tasks as needed. Sometimes after I've left work for the day, I suddenly remember something that should be on my to-do list for the next day. I immediately set a reminder in my calendar for the next day. This pop-up message will remind me to add that task to my list the next day. Make sure to assign your pop-up message a time when you know you won't be in a meeting or otherwise unavailable. Then when it pops up, you can put the task on your list and move on.

Also, throughout the day, tasks you didn't anticipate will come up. Do the same thing: add them as needed. But take a minute to fit it into your to-do list schedule. If it doesn't fit, see if you can do it the following day or ask someone else to handle it. (I'll say more about outsourcing in Chapter 7.)

2. Remind yourself of the place where you are in your list. Here's what I mean by that. I set aside a spot in the lower left-hand corner of my notebook for "place holders." If I get interrupted, I make a quick note of exactly what I was doing so I can get right back to it when time permits. This little trick has saved me time and again.

3. Make a separate column for personal stuff. There is a line down the middle of my steno pad. I use the left side for work to-dos, and I use the right side for personal info. It's pretty difficult to completely separate our personal life from our work life. Throughout the day, there may be errands, phone calls, or reminders we need to be aware of even while we're at work. So, this is where I write things like "go to the ATM" or "pick up dry cleaning."

4. Leave some room for notes. I take notes on everything: phone calls, TV shows, magazines, gossip, etc. I use the upper right-hand corner of my list paper to take little notes throughout the day. They might be anything from someone's phone number to a shoe size.

ANATOMY OF A TO-DO LIST

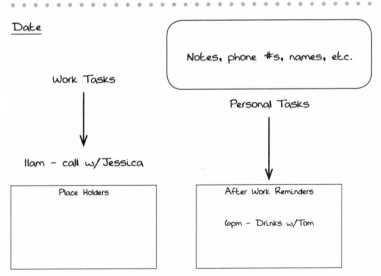

58

I also use sticky notes, but not for my to-do lists. I use them when I'm working with other people and need to give them directions. For example, when I hand off a project, I write a note like, "This is for Monday" or "Please copyedit." When I want someone to take action, I put it on a sticky note. I do use sticky notes for specific and short to-do lists though.

Pop-Up Productivity Tip

If there are two or three things I have to remember to do after work, I will write them on a sticky note and stick it to the back of my phone. Some brilliant designers actually created sticky notes that fit perfectly on an iPhone. Made by Paperback, they make list making on the go very simple. You can learn more about them at http://bit.ly/1qyWCHt.

I realize my formula for making lists at work may not suit everyone. But it's worth a try. Leah Busque, whom I mentioned earlier, is the CEO of TaskRabbit, a service that helps you get more done, and she has a different system. She makes her lists in the morning. "The first thing I do when I get into the office is sit down and develop a list of things I need to cover each day. I also develop a checklist before I go into management team meetings to ensure we hit all relevant and hot topics," she explains in a guest post on my blog.

ORGANIZING MEETINGS

Leah brings up a good topic. How do you organize meetings? With lists, of course! I've had several interns help me with my blog and this book (go to this book's Acknowledgments page to see their names in lights), and I always have a list when we chat. Taking a few extra minutes to think about your intention for your meeting will help you to focus it. How many pointless meetings have you been in, where nothing gets accomplished? It's happened to me too many times, and I literally want to lose my mind because it's so avoidable.

I wish I worked for Joe Duran, the founding partner of United Capital, an ever-growing wealth-counseling firm. The reason I think Joe has such a great work environment is he will not have a meeting without a checklist. He will turn you away if you approach him without one. I love that! "My meetings are half as long as they used to be, and I'd say they are at least twice as effective. So productivity has quadrupled on that measure," he says.

Let's be clear: a checklist is not an agenda. These are two very different tools. The items on a checklist seldom change. For Joe's staff, their checklists will include items such as updating last week's meeting items, reviewing client strategies, and going over upcoming events. Those items are on the list every single week even if there's no need to talk about them that week.

"Without a checklist it's almost impossible to have consistency. So it just assures that people do things the same way all the time," Duran explains. He first implemented the checklist system around 2010 after reading *The Checklist Manifesto*.

He was so taken with the concept that he had everyone on his staff read the book. Joe told me that there was a little pushback on the checklists at first, but now his staff embraces the process and uses checklists with their own staff. "Meetings are very crisp and tight, and they're prepared beforehand. And frankly, the act of preparing the checklist allows them to also become more disciplined as executives themselves," says Duran.

A LIST BUILT FOR TWO

Working with other people can be a task in itself. There are some tools, however, that you can use to make it easier for everyone to be accountable, focused, and productive. Meetings and check-ins about projects will help us stay on track, but there's so much more that we can do. Here are a few ideas.

1. **Assign ownership.** It's very important to be clear about who is taking care of which tasks. This needs to be done as soon as a project begins. This way there is one point person, and that is the person who will be held accountable for the good, the bad, and the ugly.

2. **Use technology wisely.** There are some programs designed to help teams work more efficiently. It's worth trying them out to see if they will help to keep your team chugging along.

Evernote

Evernote is a great tool for keeping notes, ideas, and lists in one spot. It is available on multiple platforms, such as your smartphone or your computer, and it's cloud-based so you can access information and updates anywhere.

I'm obsessed with Evernote. I use it with my interns for my blog. We have shared folders, which we all have access to. Whenever we have an idea for a blog post or see an article we like, we add it to Evernote. We also make to-do lists for each other and can easily see what tasks still need to be checked off.

I make an agenda in Evernote before every weekly call. Everyone has access to it and can add items if they'd like. This way everything we need to address gets attention. It's also nice to look back at the agenda from the week before to see if there's anything still pending that needs to be resolved.

Evernote is also a great place for collaborative writing. Sometimes I'll have an idea for a post, such as movies that incorporate lists, and I'll write a note in Evernote with ideas and movies. Then I ask my interns to do some research to fill in the blanks. When sharing notes in Evernote, be sure to assign everyone a different color font so you can keep track of who is making changes or suggestions.

Evernote is a free service, but if you want to add a business account, there is a cost. I use it for both personal (more on that in the next chapter) and business purposes, so for me it pays for itself.

Google Docs

I was a late adopter to Google Docs but it really is helpful. You can share spreadsheets and other documents with several people. It tracks who made changes and it makes it very simple to leave notes and update. I find it particularly helpful when you're editing documents and also brainstorming ideas.

Asana

There are several services like Asana that allow teams to manage their projects together. Tech expert Carley Knobloch told me about Asana when I featured her on my blog. She takes her to-do list and imports it into Asana and then assigns tasks as needed.

Asana is a dashboard for managing projects. The idea is to have staff members assigned to projects and tasks and be able to share ideas easily. When someone finishes a task, that person checks it off a list so that everyone on the team knows it's been done. Each task can be assigned a deadline as well as reminders. This is a great way to keep people accountable and check in on progress without micromanaging.

There's also a feature that allows you to send messages to each other about specific tasks, which will stay saved so that anyone can see the back and forth. It's a great way to ditch all the e-mails you're always sending and the inevitable searching for responses at a later date. You can also upload files to a certain task and create subtasks.

Subtasks are important if you're creating a checklist. Let's say you have a new client or employee, and you always do the same set of onboarding tasks. Your initial setup is always the same, and you have a checklist of all the things you run through to get that client or employee set up. You can set up subtasks and assign them to different people on your team to have them handle it.

When I get a new intern I always do the same set of tasks:

1. Create e-mail address
2. Go over tasks and responsibilities
3. Create Evernote account
4. Etc.

I can import those into Asana and assign them to other people if I need to. Everything is in one spot, easy to find, and I'll know when tasks are completed.

You can also keep information in one place. So if you need to remember passwords or usernames or FTP addresses for a specific client, this is a great place to store that information.

There are other management systems, such as Basecamp and 5pm, but I've used Asana the most.

3. **Make good use of low-tech solutions.** In the very first newsroom I worked in, we used a huge whiteboard to keep track of stories. The assignment editor would list out which stories reporters were being sent out to cover. She'd also include who their cameraperson was, their location, and their deadline. It was an easy way to get information at a glance. This sort of system might also work for you and your team for daily and long-term projects.

Handwriting to-do lists can also work. I once spoke to Lindsey Carnett, CEO and President of Marketing Maven Public Relations, and she told me that she starts to-do lists for each of her employees: "I create my master list, then have members of my team add their lists for themselves, which helps them to organize their respective teams and to prioritize tasks, making sure nothing falls through the cracks."

Did You Know?
The Zeigarnick Effect

Definition: the psychological tendency to remember an uncompleted task rather than a completed one (Source: Merriam-Webster.com).

It was named after Soviet psychologist Bluma Zeigarnick, who first developed the theory, which suggests that we are naturally driven to finish what we start.

MANAGING PROJECTS WITH LISTS

Once you have a task on your to-do list, you need to actually set that goal into motion. I suggest making another list. (I know, I know...I will single-handedly kill off millions of trees with my advice. But we can also "go digital," which I'll say more about in Chapter 8.)

Let's say your task is to write a book. That's a big to-do item (believe me, I now know) that needs to be broken down into steps. Identify every single thing that has to happen to accomplish such a task. For example:

✓ Brainstorm ideas

✓ Ask people what they think of the idea

✓ Tweak the idea

- ✓ Learn how to write a book proposal
- ✓ Write a book proposal
- ✓ Find a literary agent
- ✓ Get a publisher
- ✓ Write the book

Even when you get to the last step, you may have more sublists to make. When writing a book, you need to break down how and when you'll have time to actually write it. See what I mean? Not all to-dos are simple. Some of them need extra thought and attention. But this may be the key to actually getting things done. People often tell me, "I never check anything off of my to-do list!" This might be why; they're not setting their lists into motion. If you set your list into motion the way I'm suggesting, I'm sure you will be more successful.

Did You Know?
Yahoo CEO Marissa Mayer Is a List Maker.

She told Mashable.com that she prioritizes with her to-do list and takes inspiration from a college friend by listing things from most important to least important. But instead of getting overwhelmed by the things she hadn't finished, her friend would celebrate her never-ending list.

"If I did [get to the bottom of the list] it would be a real bummer," Mayer explained in the Mashable article, "because think about all those things at the very bottom of your to-do list that really shouldn't take time out of your day." She went on to talk about how she'd rather not spend lots of time doing unimportant tasks. (http://on.mash.to/1zdHUec)

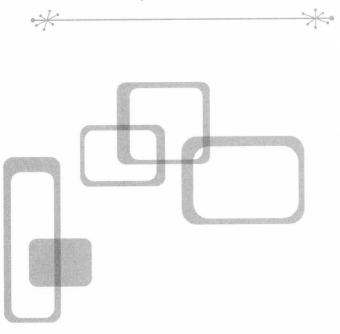

CHAPTER 5

List Sweet List:
Home Life Is Easier with Lists

Balancing the home part of life is a daily struggle. Between doctor's appointments, remodeling your kitchen, managing your finances, picking up the dry cleaning, and having enough time to make dinner, our lives are jam-packed. A little listful thinking can help us manage it all better.

First, let's talk about how to set up your day. For many of us, weekends are the only time to get home-related tasks done because we work all week. Being able to use the weekend to the fullest is essential. You must have a plan, or else the days will slip right by with a full and uncompleted to-do list.

Here's how I manage my home to-do lists. I'm much less rigid about my list making at home than I am at work. Again, I have a central notebook for all my lists. It's usually a reporter's notebook—a thin, skinny, lined book—that lives on my desk. This is where I note all the things I need to accomplish for the next day, week, and month. I capture them all in my notebook.

Then, if needed, I make separate to-do lists for each day. I usually do this on my day off so that I can tackle as much of the master list as possible. I will go through the master list and think about what needs to get done that day. If the dry cleaning has been at the store for over a week, then that's a high priority. I set up this list by deadline. Things that need to get done first go at the top, and things that aren't as important follow. That way, what I don't finish easily goes to the top of another day's list.

One of the most important parts of this task is being realistic. What can you really accomplish in the time you have available? Determining how long a task actually takes will save you time and again. You know how people always say, "I'll be there in five minutes," but don't get there until twenty? Be realistic about time, and you'll be able to get more done.

Knowing when to put the brakes on your list is important too. Not everything can get done in just one day. Health and performance consultant Heidi Hanna told me that once she realized "it's not all getting done today," her life changed. "My "enough list" gives me a chance in the morning to know that when it's noon and that list is done, I can do something relaxing or run errands or do anything else because I completed what was enough for me that day," she says.

USING LISTS TOGETHER

What about when you have to rely on other people to help you get things done? Share list making. It could be as simple as tearing a to-do list in half and giving one piece to your significant other to work on. You could also be a bit more sophisticated with your sharing.

I've already written about using the management tool Asana (see page 63) for work tasks. Well, it can also be used to manage your life at home. First, make sure everyone on your "team" has access to the same information. That will set everyone up for success, whether we're talking about picking up items at the drug store or asking questions at the pediatrician's office. There are other apps as well that can help you share your lists with others and get more done. We'll look more closely at those in Chapter 8.

GROCERY SHOPPING

If you're like me, the same things are always on your grocery list. Week after week I buy milk, English muffins, strawberries, blueberries, raspberries, apples, bananas, cold cuts, bread, etc. Every week without fail these foods make my list. So why do I write them down? So that I don't have to remember to remember them. It's a no-brainer. If you go grocery shopping without a plan, you will definitely spend more money and time.

I know you've all done it. Grabbed an avocado because it looked good and then let it sit and go bad on the kitchen counter. What a waste! Having a list will keep you on track as you navigate through the aisles. It will also make you more efficient with your time because you will be laser focused, getting in and out of the store more quickly.

Here are a few ways to make your grocery list work for you.

1. Make a list over several days. Throughout the week, my husband and I add to our grocery list as we run out of items or remember things we need. It helps to do this as soon as you realize you need something—so that you don't forget.

2. Leave your list in the same place. I leave my grocery list in a drawer in my kitchen. That way I always know where to find it when I need to update it. Although this does leave the door open for forgetting your list or not being around it when you think of something to add, I've solved this problem, which I discuss in Chapter 8, "Let's Get Digital."

I've also found that if I like the paper I'm writing on, I'm more likely to use it. If, like me, you love stationery, then this might be another motivating factor for making your grocery list.

3. Plan out meals before you go shopping. Before we walk to our local grocery store (we live in New York City, hence the walking), my hubby and I talk about what meals we want to make that week. Then we add only the items we need for those dishes to our list. That way we cut down on the aimless walking through aisles and wasting money on food we won't eat. Plus this reduces stress when you come home from work and can't think of one more thing. It makes meal prep during the week a no-brainer.

Planning out meals doesn't have to be a dreaded task. Here are a few ways to make it easier:

- ✓ Make a list of all the foods and dishes your family enjoys, so it's an easy go-to guide when you need it. Keep this list somewhere where you can find it!

- ✓ Gather recipes over time and keep them in the same place. Keep physical recipes that you pull out of magazines or print from websites in a central folder. This also works with digital recipes: keep them where you can easily find them. (I use Evernote, which I'll get into in Chapter 8.)

- ✓ Use a meal-planning service. Yep, these actually exist. Websites such as Emeals.com or TheFresh20.com will actually plan your menus and shopping lists for you for a fee. This may seem ridiculous at first, but think of all the time, energy, and stress you can save yourself. Just because you *can* do something doesn't mean you *should* do it. (More on that in Chapter 7, "Outsourcing Your Life.")

4. Grocery shop online. FreshDirect.com is my favorite shortcut of the week. You can browse their "aisles" and make lists of all the foods you need. They even have premade meals and recipes. It's a great cheat sheet, freeing up the time you would have spent walking up and down the aisles to do something much more productive.

I also make lists of commonly used ingredients in my favorite dishes. So for instance, I make turkey burgers a lot. Instead of thinking about all the ingredients that go into that dish every time, I have a premade list saved on FreshDirect.com. That way I just click once and all the ingredients I need go into my cart.

There is a delivery fee for the service, but multi-month delivery passes are also available for a discount. FreshDirect.com is only available in the New York City area, but there are other services in your area that you can find online. I also like Peapod.com, WeGoShop.com, and NetGrocer.com.

GET YOUR FINANCES ORGANIZED

Ugh! I hate numbers. Although they seriously make me anxious, I could go on and on for days about their importance. Bottom line: being organized about money will help you make smarter decisions and have more of it. If you ignore finances and hope they go away, you're only doing yourself a disservice. Just ask Suze Orman. Knowledge is power.

Remember Joe Duran, the founding partner of the wealth counseling firm United Capital, from Chapter 4? He won't have a meeting without a checklist, right? He's also the author of the New York Times bestselling book *The Money Code: Improve Your Entire Financial Life Right Now.*

It's a book about helping people make informed financial choices, and it's written in parable form. So it's a super easy read, even if, like me, you hate numbers. And it includes a checklist! Joe says the most important thing to remember with personal finances is to take emotions out of your decision making. Easier said than done right? Well, a checklist will help.

. . . .

CHAPTER 6

The Social Butterfly: Manage Your Lifestyle through Lists

One of my favorite uses for list making is planning my social life. Whether it's a party, event, trip, or even a phone call, I use lists to be better organized and make sure everything gets covered.

A LIST BETWEEN FRIENDS

Everyone has a million things going on, and sometimes it's hard to get together with your friends. But maintaining our relationships is good for our mind, body, and soul. According to the Mayo Clinic, friendships boost happiness, reduce stress, and help us cope with the hard times that come our way.

How many times have you been so excited to see someone and then left thinking, *Oh I forgot to tell you*? It's happened to me before, which is why I now make a list when I get together with friends. When I know I'm going to see a friend, I start jotting down things that I need to tell her. Sometimes I do this over time by keeping a separate page in a notebook or a list dedicated to just that person in one of my many apps. I'll include everything and anything noteworthy to tell this person. For instance, if I just found a new favorite nail polish color and I think my friend would love it, it goes on my list. Silly and serious things make the list, and it's important for me to write them down or else I'll never remember everything I want to tell.

For a while I had a group of friends who embraced my list-making ways and joined in on the fun. Whenever we would get together, we would send along an e-mail chain beforehand of all the things we wanted to share with each other the day of our get-together. We gave each item a fun title and staggered each person's items throughout the night. It was a fun and functional way to get together. I think they thought I was nuts when I first suggested it, but in the end, they ended up valuing this list making as much as I did.

Here are a few reasons why you should consider making an agenda the next time you get together with your friends or family. Making an agenda will help you to:

- ✓ **Stay on target**—especially when there's wine involved (it's easy to let the conversation wander and never get to more important stuff)

- ✓ **Remember everything**—either take a few minutes before you get together or have an ongoing list you've been keeping of the things you need to say

✓ **Create structure**—it's just one less thing you need to think about, and when a topic gets called out, that person can hit the ground running

LIST MAKING FOR PHONE CALLS

As we move forward into the digital age, the art of the phone call is dying. Research shows that eight trillion text messages were sent in 2012. That's "trillion"! Many people forgo the phone call because it's so much easier to type a few words to get your message across instead. But a little extra planning and organization can get you back on track with phone calls.

A friend of mine told me she felt bad because she never had anything to talk about with her mother when she calls. I think we've all been there. The time comes for you to talk, and your mind goes blank. This is where a list comes in handy. I suggested that my friend write down important things she wanted to tell her mother as they occurred to her—before the actual phone call. So she started making a list, and during the next phone conversation with her mom, my friend filled her mom in on everything that was going on in her life. She felt good because she really connected with her parents and her mom actually said that this was one of the best phone calls they had had in a long time. My friend let her in on the secret, that she had made a list. There's no shame in having a cheat sheet here—especially if it makes you more successful when you're talking on the phone with your mom. Try it.

PLAN THE PERFECT TRIP

Paris is one of my very favorite cities. So when my husband, Jay, and I had an opportunity to visit our friends there, we jumped at it. Nicole (the packing whiz I mentioned earlier) and Peter are New Yorkers who decided to move to the City of Lights for three months, just because they love it so much. We would be visiting them for only three days—but these would be full days. This was Jay's first visit so we really wanted to get in both the great touristy stuff and some of the off-the-beaten path attractions too.

Like me, Nicole is a planner, so we quickly got to work planning our trip. After trading a million e-mails, we narrowed down our to-do list and recorded everything in Evernote (see page 62).

- ✓ Eat fondue.

- ✓ Drink fabulous wine.

- ✓ Visit the Louvre—highlights only.

- ✓ Picnic in Luxembourg Gardens.

- ✓ Eat croissants.

- ✓ Take a Segway tour of Paris.

- ✓ Enjoy a boat tour on the Seine.

- ✓ Eat crepes.

- ✓ Watch fireworks on Bastille Day.

- ✓ Eat macarons at Ladurée.

- ✓ Enjoy a Chopin concert outdoors.

Next, we started plugging these tasks into our rundown for each day. We wouldn't be having a picnic in Luxembourg Gardens and sampling macarons at Ladurée on the same day because these locations aren't near each other. All of this had to be taken into account when laying out our plan. Our first day looked like this:

Friday

    8:30 a.m. - Land in (sometimes sunny) Paris.

    9:30 a.m. to 1:30 p.m. - Settle into hotel and nap.

    1:30 p.m. - Meet for a trip to Ladurée for Paula's first macaron; walk to 75 Rue des Champs.

    2:00 p.m. to 4:00 p.m. - Get a nice, big lunch near the hotel; walk to Café Victoria at 64 Rue Pierre Charron

    4:30 p.m. to 5:30 p.m. - Take the 1 Metro on Champs to Batobus on the Seine. Start at the Hôtel de Ville stop and end at the Eiffel Tower. Walk around the area.

    6:15 p.m. to 9:30 p.m. - Take the Segway tour. Pick up and drop off Segways near the Eiffel Tower and 24 Rue Edgar Faure.

    10:00 p.m. - Hang out to see lights at the Eiffel Tower/ Trocadéro.

    10:30 p.m. - Late dinner at Café Le Malakoff at 6 Place du Trocadéro et du 11 Novembre

End the night taking the metro or a taxi home, and get to bed!

Some people will say, "Lighten up, you're on vacation! Why schedule so much?" I totally understand what they mean, but having a rundown can save time and money. I find having a plan and doing my research beforehand is a much better way to travel. Of course, we were flexible when we needed to switch something up, but we were able to get to every single thing on our list during that short stay. We researched menus and prices and museum hours, and the trip was more relaxing this way because we'd done all the hard work ahead of time.

Pop-Up Productivity Tip
TV Producers' Secret for Time Management: Backtiming

In television news, timing is everything. Producers, anchors, reporters, videographers, and editors work on very strict deadlines. Sometimes stories have to come together quickly, which makes time management one of the keys to success in this business. Working in TV news for over a decade has conditioned me to use time management to be more efficient in my everyday life too.

Time Management
One of my time-management skills is called backtiming. It's a technique used to make sure that all the stories fit into the show so that we can get off the air on time. Here's how it works. A line producer assigns a time estimate to each story, depending on how important it is. All the time estimates are added up to fill the newscast. You have to make all the news of the day, the sports, the weather, and the entertainment fit into that time frame.

There are a lot of moving pieces in a newscast: live

shots, in-studio guests, videos from various sources, numerous reporters, anchors, sound bites, etc. Getting everything to work together is a challenge night after night. But if you've watched a nightly newscast, you know it gets done.

The Benefits of Backtiming
Backtiming is a way to count backwards. What I mean is if you have an hour to fill, then you start at the end of the newscast and work your way backwards to the top of the newscast, filling in your time cues.

While the live newscast is on the air, you have to hit specific time marks. If you don't, you know you need to make adjustments—maybe taking some time back from sports or killing that story about a cute bunny. You must be flexible to keep the newscast running on time.

Luckily, there are now computer programs that will backtime for a producer. But when I first started, this technology didn't exist. So I would backtime by hand. I hate math, but it's a useful tool.

Backtiming Your Life
How does this pertain to everyday life? Well, you can essentially backtime any task or event. I did it with my wedding ceremony, and I do it with everyday errands and when planning trips too.

Here are the steps:

1. Think about how much time you have to fill for your task or event.

2. Start from the end of the event and work your way backwards.

3. Estimate the amount of time it will take for each task.

4. Adjust those times if you find that you won't be able to accomplish everything in that time period.

5. Stick to your rundown.

This comes in handy when you're trying to get out of the house with small children—who come with a lot of stuff! To plan ahead, think about all the things you need to do to get out of the house at a specific time and then think backwards about how long each task will take you. This way, you can get out the door on time. Backtiming can be applied to just about any task or event, and it will help to reduce stress and save time because you'll be more efficient.

THE BIGGEST PARTY OF MY LIFE

As a planner I had great fun coordinating my wedding. Jay and I did a destination wedding in Puerto Rico, so researching from New York was quite a feat. Lists were my saving grace. I had one for almost everything:

- ✓ Guest list
- ✓ Research lists of vendors and venues
- ✓ Items to ship ahead of time for welcome bags
- ✓ Packing list
- ✓ Rundown for guests for the wedding weekend

Although some people will love you for having your wedding in a tropical or fun destination, be prepared for some naysayers too. Once you get over any criticism, settle on your guest list, and prepare for a lot of planning ahead of you. Staying organized when planning one of the biggest events of your life is key; otherwise, you'll be stressed and miss out on all the fun stuff!

1. Pick a destination. There are so many things to keep in mind when choosing a location for your destination wedding (or any wedding for that matter). Make sure the location you choose is accessible for most of your guests. People are going to spend a lot of money and time to get to your nuptials, so be kind to them. Do a little research to find out what kinds of activities and events they might be able to take advantage of the weekend of your wedding. You don't have to plan it all out for them, but giving your guests options is considerate.

2. Choose vendors. This is one of the toughest things to do when you're planning from far away. My best advice is to take a chance sometimes—but not without doing your homework. If you decide to go with a wedding planner (we did), it could be the some of the best money you spend on the wedding. The wedding planner lives in the area and has worked with vendors there. If you trust your wedding planner, his or her recommendations should work out just fine. You could also seek out other couples who had weddings in that area and ask them for their recommended list of vendors.

3. Interview vendors. You must go into meetings with vendors prepared, whether these meetings are on the phone or in person. Have a list of questions ready, and ask to speak to some of the brides who were their previous clients because their experiences can help you to plan the best possible event.

4. Relax. A wedding in the islands means a laid-back atmosphere. Be aware that not all of the vendors are on the same clock as you. This was very difficult for me, a Type-A New

Yorker, to grasp. I would sometimes panic, "I sent an e-mail fifteen minutes ago and still haven't heard back." Island time is island time. Learn to deal with it, and you'll be much happier.

5. Make a packing list. Preparing a thorough packing list will prevent headaches. You'll have a lot to remember, so start jotting things down early. If you need some help, I share a Destination Wedding Packing List on my blog at ListProducer.com and in the index of this book on page 142.

For any event you need to plan, whether it's a dinner party, a charity event, a birthday party, or a book club event, you'll find that planning lists will make it easier to create a successful outcome. Some people don't enjoy the events they host because they are too worried about the details. But with careful planning and well thought-out lists to guide you, you do most of the work beforehand and have as much fun as your guests at the event.

GIFT GIVING

My mother-in-law and I share a love for giving gifts, and we love shopping for them even more—but that's beside the point. She's especially good at gift giving, always finding a unique and personalized present for every occasion. It's such an amazing feeling when you give just the right gift. It makes the recipient feel appreciated and shows you care.

To find the perfect gift, it's important to think ahead. Here's a checklist for giving great gifts.

1. Start early. How many times have you waited until the last second to get a gift and either spent too much money or settled on something that was convenient but not the best gift for that person? If you start early, this outcome won't happen. Start thinking about friends' birthdays and special occasions at least two months beforehand.

I also start my holiday shopping early. Each year, I start in August. That way I can start thinking about what each person on my list would like, and I'm able to save money at different sales for Back to School, Labor Day, Columbus Day, and Veteran's Day.

2. Brainstorm. Once a month I go through my calendar to see what events or birthdays are coming up in the next few months, and I make a list in chronological order. Then I start to brainstorm for each person. I think about what that person likes, needs, or has been talking about. What would really make this person smile? This list should be an ongoing one that you can add to at any time. You can save your ideas for other events too, such as Christmas and anniversaries. Thinking ahead like this helps to reduce stress when those milestones pop up.

3. Do some research. Once you have your brainstorming list, start researching. Sometimes I take trips to different stores or visit various websites and simply take notes on items I think a friend or a relative might like. When I look through magazines and newspapers, if something interesting pops up, I write it down. Keep your list with you, and add to it during your travels.

4. Keep a log. I write down past gifts I've given people in a notebook (or in Evernote) so that I don't gift the same thing twice—unless the person really likes a certain gift, but mostly, no one wants the same gift year after year. If you have a gift log for each person you typically buy gifts for, you can avoid "repeat gifting."

I stumbled across an interesting website that I think could help a lot of people become more organized and get gifts they want. It's called MyRegistry.com, and it works just like a wedding or baby registry. You put in all the stuff you want without being tied down to just one store. You can add items from literally everywhere. How cool is that? So you could set up a registry for a housewarming, a birthday, a graduation, the winter holidays, etc. The site is not just about couples and babies, so you can get what you've always wanted and needed, even if you're single.

I'm sure etiquette mavens are gasping at the idea of asking for gifts. Ordinarily I would be doing the same thing except that this idea saves time and money. If my friends just tell me what they want for their birthday, then everyone wins! I give a gift that's wanted and don't waste time going from store to store to find something. Win-win! It's a brilliant idea.

5. Stay on budget. It's easy to get out of hand if you find a gift you really love or if you're pressed for time. But spending more money doesn't mean you're giving a better gift. Set a budget for a particular gift and stick to it. You'll be happier in the end. Let's say I see a book in a bookstore that I know my mom will love; I write down the title and try to get a better deal online if I can. When you have the luxury of time—because you started early—you can shop around and save money.

KNOWING WHAT TO SAY

We've all been there, a situation in which we're fidgeting and searching for just the right thing to say. These awkward social encounters can make us anxious, stressed, and agitated. But as with many things in life, you have to "fake it 'til you make it." Enter...the list.

Here are a few phrases and questions to bring up the next time you are at a loss for words.

Dinner Parties

For some people, dinner parties can be excruciating. Small talk, people you don't know, and awkward silences make some of us uneasy. If you go into social situations like dinner or cocktail parties prepared, though, you will have a much better time. Here are some ideas to pull you out of this tough time:

- ✓ Ask open-ended questions, not ones that can be answered with a simple yes or no.

- ✓ Compliment someone. This could spark a conversation about where the earrings you pointed out came from, which could get the ball rolling for an interesting exchange.

- ✓ Bring up current events. I would stay away from politics and religion until you know the person better, but all other subjects should generate some good banter.

- ✓ Talk about food. Ask about restaurants the person likes or places they have visited in your city. People are usually very passionate about this subject.

Baby Showers

Baby and bridal showers can be so awkward. There are a bunch of women from all parts of the guest of honor's life, but sometimes they have nothing in common. Well, at least, you would think that at first, until you break the ice:

- ✓ How do you know the mom-to-be?
- ✓ Ask what the person's favorite book was as a child.
- ✓ Bring up travel plans—this could get the conversation flowing.
- ✓ Mention a movie that has something to do with weddings or babies.

Elevators

At least once a day I used to get into the elevator at work and find myself at a loss when someone else entered from another floor. Luckily, I work at a TV station, so we have TVs running 24/7 in our elevators, which cuts down on the awkward elevator meetings. Here are some ideas if you don't have technology to help you out:

- ✓ Smile. Sometimes that's all you need to do to break the ice.
- ✓ Mention the floor where the person is going to get off and ask what is on that floor.
- ✓ Respect space. Not everyone wants to talk in an elevator. It's okay to say nothing sometimes.

Funerals

Nerves and emotions get the better of us when someone dies. If you weren't super close to the person who passed away, it can be especially difficult to know what to say. Here are a few suggestions:

- ✓ Share a fond memory or story about the deceased person.
- ✓ Simply say, "I know this is a hard time for you and your family. Please know that my heart goes out to you."
- ✓ Talk about the deceased person's accomplishments, whether in the realm of family, career, or community life.
- ✓ You might offer to clean up after the guests leave, or if you know the grieving host well enough, offer to cook dinner.

Questions to Keep on Hand

- ✓ What was the best part of your day today?
- ✓ What was the last movie you saw?
- ✓ What type of books do you like to read?
- ✓ If you could live anywhere, where would you live?
- ✓ Do you play any instruments or speak any other languages?
- ✓ What type of kid were you?

List of Things to Say If You Meet a Celebrity

In my career, I'm fortunate to have a ton of opportunities to meet interesting and influential people. Every once in a while, this includes a celebrity. When I knew I would be meeting Betty White, I was so excited because I've always been a huge *Golden Girls* fan. I actually got the chance to chat with her and even appear in a quick segment with her. It was lovely, and she was fantastic.

However, I don't always keep it so cool when I meet famous people. I've been a fan of Oprah my entire life, but when I saw Gayle King in an elevator, I completely froze. I didn't want to blurt out, "I love Oprah too!" so I said nothing.

It can be awkward.

When you meet a celebrity, you know so much about their career and often their personal lives too, but you are a complete stranger to them. No one wants to be asked about their divorce or have someone they don't know give them career advice. I imagine celebrities feel the same way. So what do you say?

I once made a list of specific questions to ask Oprah, but later I realized I needed a more general list in case I ever run into Stedman or Gayle again. To avoid being rude, embarrassing myself, or saying nothing, I came up with this list of things to say to a celebrity:

1. "I really like your work with [fill in the blank]!" So many celebrities have passion projects they care about outside of the work they're famous for. I'm sure they'd love a little recognition for projects that are close to their hearts.

2. "What do you think happened to [that character]?" Odds are, the actor who played your favorite TV character loves the character just as much as you do and has spent time speculating where that character ended up. This would have been a great question for James Gandolfini; I would love to know what he thought happened to Tony Soprano.

3. "You inspired me to [fill in the blank]." Most celebrities are artists, creating work they hope will influence people. Celebrities get told all the time how much people love their work, and while that appreciation may not get old, it might be more rewarding for them to find out they were a positive influence on someone.

4. "Have *you* ever been star-struck?" Even celebrities have celebrities they want to meet. If you're really nervous and need a way to break the ice, try calling yourself out on being star-struck. Odds are, the celebrity has a story about being nervous meeting someone too. This one might seem a little out there, but it totally worked for my intern when she met Dave Matthews.

5. "Cool necklace! Where did you get it?" This one is great for meeting a celebrity you don't know much about. Pick the most striking item he or she is wearing or carrying and ask about it.

You never know what kind of story might be behind it or what kind of conversation it may trigger.

Whatever you decide to say, remember to breathe, try not to freak out, and prepare to tell this story forever.

CHAPTER 7

Outsourcing Your Life Will Set You Free

When I get into the office on a Monday morning and ask coworkers how their weekend was, I get a similar response from many people, "Too short!" Time—it's what everyone complains about and wishes we had more of. But maybe that's because many of us are not using our time wisely enough.

Even very productive people have trouble getting everything done throughout the day. But the secret really is being able to delegate. If you can take something off your plate so that you can work on something else that you're better at, you will be much more efficient.

TOM SAWYER, THE ULTIMATE OUTSOURCER

You may remember Tom Sawyer as a troublemaker, but he was also a master at outsourcing. You can see how he used it to his advantage in *The Adventures of Tom Sawyer,* where he wanted to get out of doing his chores.

In case you don't remember the story, I'll summarize. Tom is in trouble again, and his Aunt Polly isn't happy with him. His punishment is to spend his Saturday whitewashing the fence. But Tom would rather do other things with his time, so he cleverly convinces other boys to do the work for him. He tells them what a pleasure it is to whitewash a fence and that not everyone is cut out for it. Tricked into doing Tom's work, the boys trade things like an apple, a kite, a piece of chalk, some tadpoles, marbles, a kitten with one eye, and many other trinkets for a chance to try whitewashing the fence. Three coats of paint later, Tom had quite a collection of booty without having to break a sweat.

Tom could paint the fence himself, but he didn't want to do it. Does that sound familiar? How many times have you been faced with an errand, like going to the drug store, or a task, like updating your blog, but felt pressed to find the time or the will to do it? Tom teaches us an important lesson: outsourcing will set you free!

WHAT IS OUTSOURCING?

Outsourcing is getting someone else or a service to do tasks for you, so that you free up time to do the things you're really good at. (In Tom's case this meant relaxing outside and collecting goodies!) Outsourcing also cuts down on the pressure we put on ourselves. "There's this shared kind of cultural story that the busier you are, the more stressed you are, the more important you are," Heidi Hanna points out.

I used to be a control freak about everything I had to get done at work and at home, but when I realized there was a better way, I quickly retrained my brain. Now, I think in terms of who can do some of those jobs well. Then I can focus on going to my day job, writing this book, maintaining my blog, and going to dinner with my husband. These are things that only I can do, and I'd much rather give my time to them. I could recode my website or go grocery shopping, but they're not the best use of my time.

One of the most effective and successful outsourcers I've ever met is Ari Meisel. When Ari was diagnosed with Crohn's disease, he was able to figure out a way to get off his meds and live a healthy life, with the help of his doctors. I interviewed him about his journey for my day job. I quickly found out that his experience led him to perfect "the art of less doing" in order to keep his stress levels down. Ari created LessDoing.com and wrote a book, *Less Doing, More Living: Make Everything in Life Easier*, to help people "optimize, automate, and outsource everything in life and be more effective at everything."

Ari believes that you shouldn't waste your time doing things that other people are just better at—which allows you to do what you're great at and really want to do. "Skillsets that we lack, that other people have, that we're really not best served learning ourselves and probably couldn't reach the same level of expertise are best outsourced," says Ari Meisel.

You've probably used a travel agent in the past, right? Well this is the same sort of idea. You could scour the Internet looking for the best deals and recommendations, or you could leave that to someone who could do it better. Then you can use that extra time to take on another client, who will help pay for that ziplining adventure package you want to add to your vacation.

POSSIBILITIES ARE LIMITLESS

I've been raving about the movie *Limitless* ever since Jay and I saw it in 2011. If you haven't seen it yet, you need to! Not only because Bradley Cooper is easy on the eyes but also because it's a very entertaining thriller. I guarantee that by the end of the movie you'll want the drug called NZT.

NZT allows people to access 100 percent of their brain instead of the 20 percent we normally use. It's like being your best possible self—and then some! Bradley Cooper's character, Eddie, learns languages in a fraction of the time and recalls all sorts of information and memories in a flash. He writes a novel in just days and becomes rich fast by learning the ins and outs of trading stocks.

Talk about crossing off everything on your to-do list! Wouldn't it be nice to whiz through all the things you need and want to do? Well, you can—without NZT. It's possible with outsourcing.

BENEFITS OF OUTSOURCING
. . . .

I've written a lot about how important it is to remember that you are just one person. Give yourself a break sometimes! It's not always possible to get everything done on your own, which is why sometimes you have to ask for help. I finally took my own advice and enlisted the help of some interns. Wow! Has my life gotten better. It's really amazing what giving up a little control can do.

There are major benefits that come from having an extra set of hands:

You can keep track of your ideas. Do you ever wake up in the middle of the night with a brilliant thought? Maybe you write it down, but then you lose track of the piece of paper or get caught up by your life again and forget your inspiration? When you have help, you have someone who will keep track of all your "crazy ideas" and help manage the things you forget. A simple, "Hey! You wanted to do this, how would you like to proceed?" from a helping hand will keep you focused and on track.

You will have more time. Maybe you have a great idea but no time to implement it. An extra set of hands to do research or reach out to a contact will allow you to get more done. If there's too much on your plate, get an extra fork!

You can make more money. You might be more successful if you have someone to help manage your workload and keep track of your ideas. Maybe you'll finally get to develop a new idea because you'll have the means and the assistance to get it done.

You will experience less stress. Having too much on your to-do list distracts you from really focusing on the task at hand and can diminish the quality of your work. Delegate some of what needs to get done, and you'll be less stressed and produce better work.

In *Stressaholic: 5 Steps to Transform Your Relationship with Stress,* Heidi Hanna points out, "Multitasking decreases performance and actually wastes time and kills energy and all of these negative things. People are really drawn to do it because they feel like they need to get more done in less time."

Technology goddess Carley Knobloch founded Digitwirl. com (which has morphed into CarleyK.com) because her crazy life as a life coach and mom of two was driving her into the ground. She told me that getting things off your plate that make you feel terrible is a big win. "Wouldn't I love to not have to run two extra errands so I can just stay with my kids a little bit longer or just so I don't have to feel drained after I go to Costco? I would rather pay someone to go to Costco any day of the week. It's worth it to me not just because of the money but also because of how I feel at the end of that experience. I'd just rather not feel that way," she says.

You will enjoy camaraderie. It's always good to be able to rely on someone who has your best interests and goals in mind. Hiring help will keep you balanced. You'll be able to trust an intern or an assistant to maintain your tasks and schedule, while you redirect your own brainpower. You'll have someone you can run ideas by and who'll also make sure you're taking a lunch break when you've got a particularly hectic day.

If you're still hesitant to recruit someone to help you, ask yourself the following questions:

✓ What big ideas would you launch if someone else could manage the details?

✓ What have you been meaning to do that keeps getting put on the back burner?

WHAT TO OUTSOURCE?

You will be very surprised by the number of things you can outsource in your life. The possibilities are many. I've outsourced a variety of tasks, including my grocery shopping, my housecleaning, research, blog-post formatting, and social media management.

Ari Meisel told me that he outsources just about everything including:

✓ A podcast

✓ Editing

✓ Transcribing

✓ Writing blogs

✓ Social media maintenance

✓ Research

✓ Ordering supplies

✓ Making appointments and schedules

✓ Travel planning

✓ Getting French citizenship (!)

"The things that everybody says is 'Oh it will just take a minute; I'll do it myself.' Nothing takes a minute, and those are the things that if you can get enough of those done, it really, really adds up to something special," says Ari Meisel.

Did You Know?
You Really Can Pay People to Do Any Task

In a *New York Post* article titled "NY Full of 24-Hour Lazy People," Reed Tucker details several things to outsource. He notes that for a price, you can practically delegate any task, even having someone else drive your car for you. For twenty bucks an hour, a guy from Brooklyn will drive you wherever you want to go—you just supply the wheels. (http://bit.ly/1tvY2lZ)

Here are a few ideas on other things to outsource:

1. Packing a healthy lunch for your child (Yep, there's a service that will do it: InBoxYourMeal.com.)

2. Dog walking and puppy poop cleaning

3. Decorating for a birthday party

4. Housecleaning (Leave the tile scrubbing to someone else while you organize your fall sweaters by color.)

5. IKEA furniture assembly (Let someone else figure out how.)

6. Rearranging furniture (Need to move around some large furniture pieces to make room for your Christmas tree? Hire a mover.)

7. Picture hanging (Make your home a bit more "homey" before your parents come to visit.)

8. Shopping for the gifts you need to give

9. Researching the most cost-effective ways to tour Italy

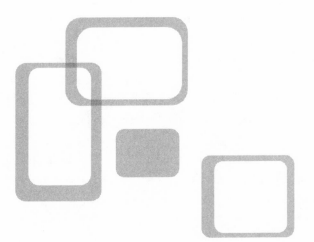

HOW TO OUTSOURCE

Have I convinced you? Let *me* help *you* find good help. Okay? The first task when hiring is to figure out who "gets" you. If you're going to use a virtual assistant to help with work tasks, it's important that you mesh. When you're delegating important aspects of your business, you want to make sure you can rely on that person. For some other tasks, though, any reputable assistant will do.

Here are a few resources to help you find the best person for the job:

1. Elance.com—great for building a workforce. Post a freelance job and hear back from qualified designers, writers, graphic artists, accountants, marketing specialists, virtual assistants, and just about any other specialty you can think of.

2. FancyHands.com—by far one of my favorite outsourcing companies. I use this service regularly, and it's been a huge help. They will do any virtual task as long as it takes about twenty minutes to complete. They will make reservations and do quick research. But they don't do physical tasks like picking up your dry cleaning or coming over to cook you dinner. Fancy Hands helped me plan a trip to Italy, research contractors, and find a guitar instructor for my husband. You pay for tasks in batches of five, fifteen, or twenty-five tasks, and they bill monthly or yearly.

3. TaskRabbit.com—another one of my favorites. This company was started because the CEO needed food for her dog but was working late. So Leah Busque dreamed up a solution. "Even

if I am marginally better at doing something, it makes sense to outsource it if my time can be better spent doing something else," she explained in her guest post on my blog.

A TaskRabbit will help you cross off to-dos like food shopping, buying a gift for your friend, and even delivering a singing telegram! You pay per task and can take multiple bids on your project. The TaskRabbits who are bidding on your task don't know how much others are willing to be paid for your task, so it's pretty competitive, and if you like a particular TaskRabbit, you can hire him or her again.

4. Handy.com (formerly Handybook.com)—a great resource for finding a cleaning service, plumber, or a handyman. The idea is to spend less time scouring the Internet for reputable and reliable service people. Think about all the time you will save Googling sites and names!

5. Guru.com—another service to help find freelancers. You can find technical, creative, and business types on this site. Whether you need an online chat specialist, a poet, or an event planner, you can find that person here.

6. Wun Wun—an app from a New York start-up that, unlike other services, specializes in deliveries. With this app, you can have anything you want delivered to you anywhere in Manhattan, the Hamptons or San Francisco. Your favorite dessert, a pair of new jeans, cases of wine for a party—you name it, they'll deliver it.

7. Zirtual.com—a sort of matchmaking site of virtual

assistants. You fill out a profile, and they pair you with the best person for the job. Then you have one dedicated assistant to help you with your tasks. Fees start at $99 a month. The virtual assistants can help with research, scheduling, purchasing, data entry, e-mail processing, phone calls, and much more.

8. Hire an intern—interns are usually free labor. Interns are also probably doing schoolwork along with your projects, so they're not dedicated solely to you. I've had several amazing interns help me maintain my blog, research this book, and handle my social media. I chose interns who are interested in my industry. I've given them tours of studios, introduced them to experts, critiqued their résumés, and given them career advice and guidance. I happen to like doing all those things, but they are time-consuming. So even though you are getting "free" help, if you're good to your interns, it will be a bit of a time investment as well. Keep that in mind. The process of finding someone can be a bit of a challenge as well, but once you find that person, the payoff is immense. I put an ad on Linkedin.com and reached out to local universities with internship programs.

HOW MUCH?

Now, the part you've been waiting for: how much will outsourcing cost me? Well, first thing about this is, what is it worth *to you* to have help? I believe that if you can do just one more project per month, with a little assistance, the investment is well worth it.

Ari Meisel told me that he has saved 3,000 hours and half a

million dollars over the last two years because he's outsourced so many tasks. Those numbers are staggering. Let's be realistic: this is all a bit subjective because it depends on how much you value your time, what your own personal skill set is, and how much money you have. But really, wouldn't you rather have 3,000 hours to play with your kids or lay on a beach instead of running errands? That half a million could come in handy too!

Here's another idea: how about bartering for assistance? When you barter, you trade services with someone who can help you out. So for instance, I could write copy for a web designer's personal website, and in return, she could make me a new logo for my website. See how that works? You can use something you're good at to get something you need—without money ever exchanging hands. This option is more time-consuming, so decide what makes the most sense for you.

HOW TO DELEGATE

In theory it's an amazingly freeing thought to give your chores to someone else. But unlike Tom Sawyer—not everyone has such an easy time delegating—it definitely takes some practice. Here are a few tips:

1. Be organized. Write a list of all of the things you can delegate. Be super specific. This list might include scheduling appointments, coming up with menu ideas for dinner, picking up items for an upcoming party, managing an overflowing e-mail inbox, and redesigning blog logos, among a variety of tasks.

2. Be realistic. You know yourself better than anyone, so be honest about what really takes five minutes to do and what can be outsourced.

3. Be humble. Don't try to be a superhero and do it all. That idea is so passé. Be smart about what you're good at and stick to that.

4. Be clear. Ari makes a checklist of every process he has his virtual assistants complete for him. He has fifty-three checklists at this point, for all sorts of tasks, including paying bills. The more work you do upfront to make sure that your hired help understands the task, the more seamless the transition will be.

5. Be grateful. Now that you have extra time to do the things you really want to do, smile! You've effectively outsourced things that you could have done yourself but didn't need to. Now you can spend more time with your family, go on vacation, read a magazine, or take a nap. Relish it!

CHAPTER 8

Let's Get Digital

I have a confession to make. I was a latecomer to the digital world, and I thought apps were stupid. There, I said it. I had a tiny flip phone for way too long and just couldn't wrap my mind around the necessity of an app for anything. And I certainly couldn't figure out why it was such a big deal that I had to tap thirteen times to type out the five-letter word "hello" on my trusty "not-smart" phone. Frankly, I was turned off by the iPhone and thought my little flip did everything I needed it to—ring and connect me with whomever I wanted to talk with. I also had my paper and pencil for all my list-making needs, thank you very much.

But after much nudging from my husband, I finally made the switch to an iPhone, and I will say it: I was totally wrong on this one. I do not know how I lived life without it. It's beyond amazing for keeping track of everything in my life and helping me do more in less time. So if you're a holdout like I was, please give it a shot, a real shot, and I promise you will see the value in all things digital as well.

PROS AND CONS OF GOING DIGITAL

I still make my handwritten lists, but digital lists and apps are a much needed complement to being more productive. Turns out I'm not alone on that front. A study conducted by Forrester Research for Livescribe, the makers of digital smart pens, found that professionals use laptops and tablets for their work needs, but 87 percent of them use handwritten notes too.

There are pros and cons, of course, to moving your list making to the latest technology. Here are a few of them:

Pros

✓ **You can sync.** Most of the apps that you'll use will sync over multiple platforms so that you can access your list anywhere at anytime. This means if you write a list on your desktop on a website it will also be on your smart phone when you leave work and head to the grocery store.

✓ **You won't lose notes.** One of the top complaints about writing lists on paper is that people lose them. Not anymore! When you use technology, your lists will be stored for the long haul.

✓ **You'll revisit your lists.** Often when you're writing out your bucket list or your packing list, you'll lose track of which notebook you put it in. But if you have digital lists, you are much more likely to find them easily, check them out again, and actually use them.

✓ **Searching will be easy.** No matter when or where you wrote that list, you'll be able to find it. There will be a digital record that you can pull up anytime.

✓ **You'll enjoy some great conversation.** People love talking about apps. They love to share them, they love to Google them, they love to show them off. You'll be in the know if you have a few good ones to chat about too.

Cons

✓ **Handwriting boosts brainpower.** You may not get the same mental bang for your buck as you would if you were to handwrite your list. Studies show that writing by hand helps with idea expression and improves fine motor-skill development. It's even been shown to keep aging baby boomers' brains sharp.

✓ **Technology can be overwhelming.** I get it, because I thought the exact same thing. Why would I download an app when I can just write down the note I need?

✓ **Creativity can get squashed.** If you like to draw pictures, diagrams, or tables when you take notes or make lists, it may be a bit more difficult to do digitally.

✓ **You need to do your homework.** Not every app will do what you need it to do, and not every app I love will work for you. The secret is to try it out and find which apps best serve you. This can be time-consuming and sometimes frustrating, but when you find the right app, it's life changing.

Now that I've laid out the pros and cons, I have to tell you that all of the cons can be overcome. You don't have to give up your pens and paper just yet. There are ways to use digital and traditional list-making methods together, and there are wonderful benefits to be had going digital. When I chatted with technology expert Carley Knobloch, she told me that using technology has been a game changer for her as a mom. "Now I have a place where I can capture fleeting thoughts that are going to absolutely leave my brain if I don't shortly capture them. There is just too much happening, too much going on," she said.

TAME THAT TO-DO LIST

For those of you who think you've found the perfect to-do list app with the Notes app on your iPhone, I urge you to use some of the following suggestions. There is life outside of that Notes app! The secret is to use many of them and to find the one that will do exactly what you need it to do to make your life easier. Some will remind you of tasks, others will make it easy to share with friends, and still others will ride you until you check off items. Find one that works for you.

Here are a few of my favorites:

Evernote. If there is only one app you download in your lifetime, make it Evernote. As I mentioned in Chapter 4, Evernote can be used when working with other people because it makes collaboration a snap. But it's also a wonderful tool when you're handling everything yourself. It's incredibly versatile, whether you use it to help manage your expenses at work or to plan the perfect birthday party for your kids.

In addition to downloading the app, you can log onto their website, Evernote.com, and access all your notes on a desktop, laptop, or tablet just about anywhere. Evernote is a cloud-based system where you can keep just about anything you want: notes, photos, website clippings, and even audio files. A friend who is also obsessed with it once called it an "extension of her mind." I think that's pretty accurate. Anything you want to keep track of but might forget should go into Evernote. And you can create multiple notebooks to keep all your ideas organized.

Here's how I'm using it:

Outlines and Ideas. Ideas for blog posts, stories to cover for work, writing projects, etc.—these pop into my head at the weirdest times. But now I can open Evernote on my iPhone anytime and jot down whatever I'm thinking about and follow up later. I also make outlines for scripts and blog posts when I'm commuting so that when I get to a computer I can be more efficient.

Web Clippings. Evernote has this cool bookmark feature for your browser; when you click on it, it saves the page you're looking at. So if you want to save a recipe, an article, or a gift idea, just click on the little elephant icon, and it'll do all the work for you.

Vacation Prep and Research. Whenever I plan a vacation, I do it in Evernote. It's an organized system that keeps all my documents together. You can send an e-mail to your personalized Evernote account, and your documents, travel information, and itinerary will automatically be saved. Then you can put them all together in a notebook for easy access while you travel. These notes can be downloaded right to your phone, so you won't need to worry about having Wi-Fi to access them.

I also compare vacation spots, resorts, and more using a note in Evernote, and I keep these so I can always refer back to them. For example, every November my husband and I try to go away someplace warm. I do lots of research on multiple locations every year. My comments and the pros and cons on each resort are saved in Evernote so that the next time we're planning a trip I don't have to start from scratch.

Record Interviews. If you need to record a conversation or a speech, you can do it right into Evernote. There is an option to record audio, and it comes in handy more than you think it might. If you're at a conference, you can take notes or just record it. I've captured audio from interviews I've conducted over Skype using this feature too. You can also drag preexisting MP3 files into a note and store them that way.

Passwords. You can keep all your passwords in a note so you'll never forget them again. You can even put a password on this note in case you want added protection.

Note-taking. Whenever I go to a conference, I take all my notes during sessions using Evernote. I'm able to take photos of the presenters, record the audio of their speeches, and type out notes too. I even use it to make a list of important contacts I make and how I need to follow up with them when the conference is over. Evernote makes this much more manageable for me.

List Keeping. I've been known to keep a few to-do lists and restaurant lists in Evernote. But for the most part I use other apps for these specific tasks.

Holiday Shopping. This is probably one of the most consistent uses I have for Evernote. Each year I make a list (in August) of all the people I need to buy holiday gifts for. Then I write in some ideas I already have and add to that list later when something occurs to me, wherever I am. Evernote makes it easy to keep track of everyone on my list and to check people off when I'm finished with them. I also use the web-clipping tool to save gift ideas throughout the year. When I'm stumped on what to get, I just refer to my notebook in Evernote and find inspiration.

Having Trouble Making Evernote Work for You?

People tell me all the time that they've downloaded Evernote but could "never get into it." I get that. Evernote does require a little bit of a commitment at first before it can be really useful. Here is my list of tips and tricks to help make Evernote one of the best things that's ever happened to you.

1. Use it often. The more you use it, the more useful Evernote becomes. Believe me. Notes in Evernote last forever, unlike that Post-it® stuck to your cell phone. When you can go back through weeks of to-do lists and breathe easy because you didn't miss a single thing, you'll know what I mean.

2. Download the Web Clipper. It will become second nature to clip all the things you want to save. Anything you can think of will be easy to stow away, like an article you want to read later, a job you want to apply to, or an idea for a Christmas gift for your mother. It works on any website you visit, and there's even a handy way to write yourself notes and tag them so you can easily find them when you need them.

3. Sharing is caring. The ways you can use Evernote to collaborate are endless. If you're planning a wedding far from your bridesmaids, start a folder to keep ideas. Then each of you can add to it and comment on the things you like and don't like. The Web Clipper makes it super simple. Try this when planning events, vacations, collaborating on blog posts, and so much more.

4. Use the e-mail feature. Every Evernote account comes with a personalized e-mail address. Use it. It is a great time saver. When you get a confirmation that you want to keep track of, such as the receipt of a gift you've purchased, send it to your Evernote e-mail. It will automatically be placed in your notebook, making it easy to access whenever you need it.

I also use this feature when making charitable donations or paying professional organization fees. When the e-mail confirmations come, I forward them to my personalized Evernote e-mail account and save them as the tax write-offs they are for that year. Everything is nice and neat and in one spot. I could go on and on and continue this list forever because there are so many ways to use Evernote. And the truth is I'm finding new uses all the time. But my best advice to you is to just start using it. The more you use it, the more you'll think of it as a second brain, and the more useful it will become.

Clear—Tasks, Reminders and To-Do Lists. Clear is by far one of the most beautifully designed apps you will ever use. It's very clever and user friendly. It will make you want to add things to your to-do lists.

Here are the pros and cons I see for Clear:

Pros

1. Stunning design

2. Easy and fun to use—swipe to delete or complete, drag to reorder tasks, etc.

3. Cute sound effects (if you're into that type of thing)

4. Simple way to keep your to-do list organized

5. Use of colors to prioritize tasks

6. Great place to keep track of lists of things, such as lists of restaurants to try, books to read, or tasks to do on a specific day

Cons

1. Can only view ten tasks at a time

2. Can be a little confusing when jumping between the layers of menus

I use this app to keep track of blog post ideas, long-term goals, and quick shopping lists. It's definitely worth a look. A common complaint, however, is that it's a bit too flashy.

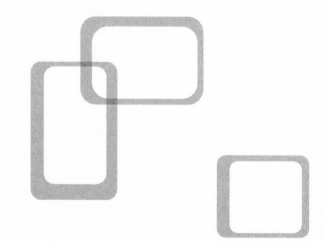

Carrot To-Do. I don't usually respond well to bullies, but for some reason I like the pushy ways of this app. The idea is that this to-do list with a personality will help you get all your tasks checked off. And when I say "personality," I mean "attitude." Carrot's mood changes depending on how productive you are. It's pretty funny actually. As you finish a task, you earn points and unlock new features and rewards.

Here's my list of pros and cons for Carrot:

Pros

1. The fun game-type format makes you want to complete tasks to find out what Carrot has in store next.

2. It's very easy to use and intuitive.

3. One of the gifts it gave me was a cat named Captain Whiskers. How cute!

Cons

1. Not a very forgiving app if you make a mistake at first. As you work your way through the levels, however, you are able to edit, undo, and change tasks.

2. I could see people getting tired of Carrot's shtick and not using it after the novelty wears off.

I think this could be a fun way to get more done for a lot of people. It's definitely worth a try.

Wunderlist. This is a great app for organizing your to-dos or lists. I use it when I'm making a quick trip to the grocery store or the drug store. It's easy to get distracted by the shiny things you encounter at the store, but this app will keep you on track. I like it for short lists. It's pretty simplistic—but anything is better than the Notes app on the iPhone!

Any.DO. I like this one because it is also a calendar, so you can easily set deadlines and invite people to help you check off some of your to-dos. The other nice feature is that you can write notes inside your to-dos. So if you have an item like "make dinner," you can add notes with ingredients right inside that item. Carley Knobloch points out that it will help you identify free time and suggest things on your list that you can do with that time. Talk about managing your day!

Todoist. Priority is the name of the game with this app. You can prioritize each to-do, file them in different projects, and make subtasks if needed. I like this one because it has a lot of flexibility. It's not simplistic, like some of the others, but it's also not complicated. There are also many plugins for Gmail, Outlook, and several browsers and computer systems to help you integrate your task mastering. Use the features that work best for you and ignore the others. It's ideal for the novice as well as the seasoned list maker.

SAVE YOUR FAVORITE LISTS

I told you all about catalog lists in Chapter 2. These are the lists we keep of things, not tasks. Sometimes having a specific app for each of the things (books, restaurants, birthdays, etc.) you want to remember is the way to go because then you know exactly where to find those lists.

Goodreads. Are you always looking for book recommendations? I love Goodreads because you can link up with friends who like the same kinds of books you like and get their recommendations easily. I also like it because it's where I keep all the books I want to read. People tell me about great books all the time, but if I don't write them down, I'll never remember them. Instead of writing them down on a piece of paper that I might lose or file somewhere on another app, I save books in Goodreads because it's only for managing book lists.

Birthdays. There are several apps that help you manage all the birthdays, anniversaries, and special days you need to remember. I use a very simple one called Birthdays, which links with Facebook and imports all the birthdays and photos of my friends and family. Using an app like this is a good practice because this is the only information you'll be keeping there so you'll never forget where to find it.

Matchbook. Matchbook allows you to enter the name of any restaurant or store you want to remember. In the old days you used to take an actual matchbook to write down and remember your favorite spot; now you save it to the Matchbook app. You can also add tags to remember certain things about a place—like if it's got a great brunch, is loud, or is super trendy. If you're stumped for a spot to meet friends after work, you can search via neighborhood and tags.

Matchbook works all over the world and organizes your bookmarks by area, which makes it easy to find a place quickly. There's also a map so you can see your bookmarks laid out in front of you and see what's closest to you. You can share places with friends, but you don't have to "friend" anyone through the app. Matchbook will help you with lots and lots of list making.

Dashlane. This is an app dedicated to saving all your passwords. It's much more secure than writing your passwords on a sticky note or storing them on your computer. Plus it will help you come up with more powerful passwords based on the ones you use everyday. Think about all the times you've been locked out of your accounts because you forgot your password. This app is a must-have for anyone managing multiple accounts—and who isn't these days?

MANAGE YOUR MONEY

Most of us want to put our head in the sand when it comes to managing our finances. But ignoring your bills won't make them go away. So my advice is to be out in the open with all of it, and get the right tools to help you deal.

Mint. This is a great way to stay on top of your finances without doing much work at all. All you have to do is link your bank accounts, any investments, and any loan information, and Mint keeps track of everything for you. It will keep those accounts up to date and allow you to see them all at once with just one password. It will even categorize all your expenses to show you where you're spending the most money and give you suggestions for ways to save. It's a wonderful way to be reminded when a payment is due and to check your accounts at a glance. It's much easier than signing into multiple accounts. The website and app sync, so you can check out your accounts anywhere.

Expensify. This is a wonderful app for keeping track of all your expenses for work and submitting them right to your boss. When you purchase something, whether using a credit card or cash, you import that information into the app. You can even take photos of the receipts and attach them to the expense report. It makes this tedious task—dare I say it—fun!

OneReceipt. You will never save another receipt again with this app. You can snap a photo of all your receipts and keep track of purchases. It allows you to make different categories for work, home, health, travel, and so on so you can monitor spending. It will even keep track of your e-receipts and allow you to link up your e-mail account so you don't even have to remember to add information.

SHOP 'TIL YOU DROP LISTS

I've always been a shopper and pride myself on sniffing out a good deal. However, now there are tools and tricks to help us do this better. From remembering where you left your grocery list to making sure all your coupons are in one place, there's definitely an easier way to do it. Apps are your answer.

ZipList. This app makes food prep easier, one list at a time. ZipList's app and website let you browse recipes and quickly add all the ingredients to your shopping list. It makes listing everything you need at the grocery store a snap. You can also import your own lists and save recipes from other websites as well as your own family favorites. Plus you'll never experience the frustration of forgetting your grocery list at home again!

CardStar. Keychains are for keys, and CardStar is for your loyalty cards. This is a great way to keep all your loyalty and discount cards in one easy-to-find place. Just scan each one and then pull it off your keychain forever. The app will even let you know when a particular store is having a sale or has a coupon available.

Slice. This is one of my favorites around the holidays because I do so much online shopping. Slice syncs with your e-mail account so that whenever you get a confirmation on a purchase, the app will track the delivery for you. You'll get friendly little reminders when the package is out for delivery and when it makes it to your door. Not having to remember which order is coming on which day is a huge time saver. As if that weren't enough, Slice also alerts you when the price of something you just bought drops, and it will help you get money back when that's possible. Finally, Slice will also alert you when the Consumer Product Safety Commission has recalled a product.

PLANNING MADE EASY

For a short time I had a party-planning business with a friend of mine. I guess it stemmed from my love of organizing things and my enthusiasm for putting together perfect events. I get that not everyone loves the task of planning outings, vacations, and parties. So, why not embrace technology to give you a helping hand? I use Evernote for a lot of my planning as I mentioned earlier, but there are other great tools as well.

TripIt. Put all of your travel plans in one place with this app. Your account is linked to your e-mail so that when you get confirmation for upcoming travel, it's added right into TripIt for you. So, your flight information, car service confirmations, hotel bookings, and more are all in one place. The app will even give you directions to get from one stop to another, which I love because then I know exactly how long it should take to get from the airport to the hotel.

There's also a website where you can manually enter information. You can forward messages right to your personalized TripIt e-mail and import anything else you'd like to add, such as tour information or that pasta-making class you signed up for. If you upgrade to their premium service, TripIt will notify you if your flight has changed and what gate you'll be leaving from. It's a time saver and a headache reducer in every way.

Pro Party Planner. Planning a party can be a huge undertaking. If the thought of organizing a bar mitzvah, sweet sixteen, or wedding makes you cringe, then this is the app for you. You can create a timeline linked to the tasks you need to accomplish with their deadlines. A budget feature will keep you informed of how much you've already spent and how much money you still have for your party. The task management tool allows you to outsource each task and check in with the people helping you via e-mail, text, or even FaceTime. There's even a seating arrangement tool.

IT'S FUN TO SHARE

Keeping up with your family can be a job in itself. Appointments, events, classes, your kid's sports commitments and dance classes—these all fill up your life, but they can be tough to organize in one place.

Hatchedit. This is an app and website that handles your family's calendar. You can share it with several people, such as your significant other, baby sitter, or dog walker. The site will help you keep track of upcoming events, invitations, daily to-dos, favorite blogs, and groups you're a part of. So whether you want to plan an event with your book club or your child's soccer team, all the information can be stored and shared. When you sign up, you get your own dashboard, which you can easily make a part of your everyday routine. If you're drowning in paper calendars or want to ditch your dry erase board, this is a great way to organize your life.

Cozi. One-stop shopping will organize everyone in your home. Cozi allows you to share lists of tasks or items to get at different stores with family members. It will also sync with your calendar so that you can keep track of where everyone needs to be. Each family member gets a color. There's even a journal where you can share photos and thoughts with your "inner circle." Another nice feature is that you can share this journal with people who aren't on Cozi by sending them an e-mail or setting up a monthly newsletter of updates. It's a cute way to keep your family members in the know.

EMBRACE YOUR INNER TOM SAWYER

As I mentioned in the last chapter, I'm all about outsourcing the tasks I don't need to do so I can focus my attention else-where—not unlike Tom Sawyer and his painting project. There are some pretty great apps and services out there that will handle the to-dos that you'd rather not.

Path Talk (formerly TalkTo). Never waste time again on the phone with a customer service rep, searching for a shoe at a store, or changing an appointment. Path Talk is an app that lets you text any business in the United States and ask them a question. It conveniently helps you reserve a table, find out if an item is in stock, find out what a store's hours are, compare prices, and so much more. My requests were responded to in as fast as five minutes. My favorite part is that you can put in a request and then forget about it. Even if the question comes to you in the middle of the night, you can just send it to Path Talk, and once the store or restaurant opens, it will be addressed.

Fancy Hands. I've been a big fan of FancyHands.com since they first launched. It's like having a personal assistant at your fingertips. For a price, you are given a certain number of tasks per month that you can delegate—things like researching the best restaurants in Rome, booking a car service to the airport, locating a guitar teacher in New York City, and just about any task that can be done using a phone and a computer. They won't pick up your laundry, but they'll find the best service that will help you get it done.

TaskRabbit. Another of my favorite services. This app and website links you up with people in your community who will go grocery shopping for you, deliver a birthday gift to your mother, or even assemble your furniture. TaskRabbits will bid on your task, and you can check out reviews on their previous projects. I've used it to log phone interviews, set up an inventory of blog posts, and deliver a gift.

Asana. I began using Asana with my interns for my blog. It's a web and mobile service, designed by Facebook employees to improve the company's productivity. We like it because it has allowed us to send fewer e-mails, and it never lets us busy ladies forget anything! You can work on multiple projects at once with the same team and create specific tasks within each project. You can easily assign different tasks to different team members. The mobile application features notifications that let you know when it's time to complete a task. You can use it at home too—say goodbye to chore charts forever! It allows you to see what everyone is working on without nagging! The service is free for teams with fifteen or fewer members.

YOU BECOME WHAT YOU BELIEVE

As a huge fan of bucket lists, vision boards, and gratitude, I believe you can't set anything positive into motion without envisioning it first. And yes, there are digital solutions to help you live a more positive life too.

MyLifeList.org. Sharing your dreams and goals is simple with this site. Simply write out all the things you've wanted to do and then answer a few questions to help you achieve that goal. This online community shares your goals with others who can talk about their own experiences or who share the same dream. Imagine linking up with someone who also wants to travel to India to practice yoga. It's a great motivational site, inspiring you to achieve your goals.

DreamItAlive.com. If you've ever made a paper vision board, you know there's a bit of assembly required. But a virtual one is pretty simple. This website allows you to scroll through hundreds of pictures for inspiration and then attach photos of your goal. I never realized how much I wanted to make homemade pasta until I saw how happy it made someone else. The site features a community where you can share support with others. It's a great source of motivation! You can even help fund someone else's goal or ask for help with your own.

Pinterest.com. I could get lost for hours on this site. If you haven't already gotten hooked I suggest giving it a try. Type in anything that interests you, maybe visiting China, and the inspiration will surround you. Make your own boards with your aspirations and refer back to them often.

Gratitude Journal at HappyTapper.com. What a wonderful way to end your day, with a gratitude list. At first it can be a bit of a task, but once you get the hang of it, this will be extremely therapeutic. Think of all the things that you are thankful for—big and small. I'm talking about things like a quiet office, make-up sex, bagels, free lunch, intelligent conversation, or walking in the park. Anything and everything that makes you smile should go into this journal. And studies show it will make you happier to be more grateful.

PIXELS VS. PAPER

If you're still on the fence about going digital, here are a few solutions to satisfy both your need to handwrite your lists and your curiosity about going digital:

Livescribe. This company makes a lot of different pens that come equipped with a camera. So you write your notes and lists as you normally would, but it's all captured digitally too. The catch is that you need to use their special paper to write your notes. This can be a bit annoying, but the technology is super cool and worth a try. The notes sync up with an app that goes with the pen, and you can export those notes to Evernote.

Boogie Board. These tablets are perfect for list makers of all ages. They also sync with Evernote and social media platforms so that you can share your work. Think about all the doodles, lists, and charts you could write and keep track of. If you are notorious for losing your notes, this e-writer is a good solution for you. It's an ecofriendly way of taking your written notes and turning them into something digital to use.

ONE TECH AT A TIME

I do hope these solutions have inspired you to get digital. Two words of caution, though: go slowly. You don't want to blow out your technology tendons too quickly. Carley Knobloch says, "A one thing at a time approach that helps you gain confidence and build habit as opposed to trying to get everything synced and everything done and changing your whole life and all your systems just doesn't work. People fail that way, and then you're taking steps backwards in confidence."

Happy digital list making!

LAST LIST

Okay, now you know all about lists. So now what? Well, another list, of course!

1. Just start listing. It's always hardest to get started. I like to tell people to make a bucket list first. You know yourself better than anyone, so write down all the things you'd love to do if money, time, and responsibilities were no object.

2. Figure out what works for you. It's not always easy at first, but believe me, it's worth it. Try different notebooks, apps, pencils, pens, etc. One system will work for you.

3. You can list as much or as little as you like—no pressure.

4. Visit my site for list-making inspiration: ListProducer.com.

5. I've compiled a toolbox to get you started with your list making. Check out the free downloads at ListProducer.com/ListfulThinkingGuide.

6. Drop me a line if you have any questions, dilemmas, or just to say hello: paula@listproducer.com.

· ·

This index contains many of the lists I mentioned throughout this book. I hope you'll use them as a reference and a jumping off point to make your own customized lists. For more lists like this visit my site, ListProducer.com.

Apartment Search Checklist
My List Producer journey began with this checklist. So I thought it only appropriate to share it with all of you. It can be customized, but it's really the preparation you do before you step foot into a potential home of yours that will help you most.

APARTMENT SEARCH	
Address (including floor if appropriate):	
Contact:	
Number of Bedrooms:	
Square Feet:	
Rent:	
Nearest Subway Stop:	
Security:	
Laundry Facilities:	

Dishwasher:	
Lease Length:	
Available Date:	
Doorman:	
A/C:	
Utilities Included:	
Parking Available:	
Super in Building:	
Number of Closets:	
Carpet or Wood Floors:	
Freshly Painted:	
Cable Ready:	
Pets:	
Outdoor Space:	
View:	

Destination Wedding Packing List

Media

- ✓ Cell phone and charger
- ✓ Digital camera, batteries, memory cards
- ✓ iPod/MP3 player and headphones
- ✓ eReader
- ✓ Travel guide(s)

Medical

- ✓ Antibiotic cream
- ✓ Anti-diarrheal medication
- ✓ Band-Aids
- ✓ Birth control
- ✓ Bug repellent
- ✓ Extra pair of eyeglasses
- ✓ 1% Hydrocortisone anti-itch cream
- ✓ Lubricant
- ✓ Pain reliever
- ✓ Prescription medicines
- ✓ Sea-sickness bands or pills (for cruises)

Money and Documents

- ✓ Business cards
- ✓ Cash
- ✓ Driver's license
- ✓ Emergency numbers
- ✓ Itinerary
- ✓ Marriage license
- ✓ Paper airline tickets or eTicket confirmation
- ✓ Passport
- ✓ Pre-paid phone card
- ✓ Sign-in or guest book for wedding
- ✓ Items for welcome bags

Miscellaneous and Extras

- ✓ Antibacterial gel
- ✓ Cotton swabs
- ✓ Keys
- ✓ Lint roller
- ✓ Massage oil
- ✓ Plastic Ziploc® bags
- ✓ Playing cards
- ✓ Sunglasses
- ✓ Sunscreen/SPF
- ✓ Umbrella
- ✓ Groom/Bride gifts

His Stuff

- ✓ Wedding attire
- ✓ Athletic or walking shoes
- ✓ Belts
- ✓ Boxers/Briefs
- ✓ Casual shirts
- ✓ Dress shirts
- ✓ Dress shoes
- ✓ Hat
- ✓ Pants

- ✓ Pajamas/Robe
- ✓ Sandals
- ✓ Shorts
- ✓ Sports jacket
- ✓ Swimwear
- ✓ Tie(s)
- ✓ T-shirts/Undershirts
- ✓ Workout clothes
- ✓ Men's toiletries
- ✓ Comb/Brush
- ✓ Deodorant
- ✓ Floss
- ✓ Lip balm
- ✓ Shaving kit/Shaving cream
- ✓ Shampoo/Conditioner/Styling products
- ✓ Toothbrush/Toothpaste/Mouthwash

Her Stuff

- ✓ Wedding attire
- ✓ Other clothing and accessories
- ✓ Bathing suit(s)
- ✓ Bras
- ✓ Panties

- ✓ Lingerie
- ✓ Jewelry—earrings, necklaces, bracelets
- ✓ Dresses
- ✓ Heels
- ✓ Pareu/Sarong/Big scarf
- ✓ Robe
- ✓ Sandals
- ✓ Shorts/Capris
- ✓ Skirt(s)
- ✓ Slacks
- ✓ Sneakers or walking shoes
- ✓ Socks
- ✓ Stylish shirt
- ✓ Sweater
- ✓ Straw or wide-brimmed hat
- ✓ Tanks/Halters/Sleeveless tops
- ✓ Thongs
- ✓ Workout clothes

Sundries

- ✓ Baby powder
- ✓ Blow dryer/Straightening iron
- ✓ Comb/Brush

✓ Cosmetic case/Makeup bag

✓ Deodorant

✓ Foot deodorant (actually helps to minimize cuts from sandals)

✓ Makeup case

✓ Makeup remover

✓ Facial cleanser

✓ Moisturizer/SPF

✓ Tampons

✓ Liners

✓ Toothbrush/Toothpaste/Mouthwash

✓ Dental floss

✓ Shampoo/Conditioner/Styling products

✓ Hair ties

✓ Tweezers

✓ Earrings

✓ Headpiece

✓ Veil

✓ Wedding shoes

Must-Have Items to Pack When You Travel

Traveling can be very stressful no matter how much you plan. But there are some tips and tricks that I've found help. I've traveled quite a lot with my friend Nicole, whom I've mentioned before. We teamed up to write this list of travel must-haves.

Apps

- ✓ Busuu (to translate simple phrases when you're abroad)
- ✓ The Layover (to learn about Anthony Bourdain's fave spots, if applicable, in your travel zone)
- ✓ Trip Advisor (for last-minute restaurant reviews when you're on the go)
- ✓ New Pilates (for mini hotel-room workouts sans a hotel gym)
- ✓ Compass (so you always know what direction to walk)
- ✓ Weather Channel (preload your destination so you'll never get caught in the rain)
- ✓ Evernote (for all your itineraries, saved notes, directions, etc.)
- ✓ TripIt (to keep track of all confirmation numbers and a chronological look at your day)
- ✓ Next Issue (a way to keep your favorite magazines on your iPad instead of lugging them with you)
- ✓ PressReader (stay on top of the news from anywhere in the world with your favorite newspapers)

Clothes and Accessories

- ✓ Cashmere wrap for the plane
- ✓ Tieks for walking and easy packing
- ✓ Lightweight rain jacket
- ✓ A neutral wristlet for evening
- ✓ Mini umbrella
- ✓ Slippers for hotel rooms and airplane
- ✓ Crossbody purse with lots of pockets
- ✓ Eye mask for the plane

Electronics

- ✓ Splitter for headphones (so two can watch a movie)
- ✓ Headphones
- ✓ An iPad or other tablet with a keyboard case

Other

- ✓ Space Bags®
- ✓ A bright luggage tag
- ✓ Travel pillow
- ✓ Truvia® packets (to avoid chemical influx abroad)
- ✓ A pen and a mini notepad (to write down recommendations or directions)
- ✓ Mini disinfectant spray for the hotel room's phone, remote, etc.

✓ A separate bag to keep dirty laundry

✓ Plastic baggies (you never know when you might need them)

Toiletries

✓ Disinfectant wipes (individually wrapped)

✓ Mini misters (to keep your skin hydrated during flight)

✓ Mini lip balms in various tints

✓ Roll-on perfume vials

✓ Blister block (a mini deodorant for your feet that also helps to prevent blisters)

Six Free Ways to Make Someone's Day

Here's a list of gestures you can use to improve someone's day for free.

1. Smile. It's simple. I've started doing this whenever I talk to someone. Sometimes it feels forced, but I always do it. When ordering at the deli or walking into a building with a doorman, I smile at the person helping me. Instantly, it brightens their face too.

2. Take that flyer. If you're a New Yorker like me, you know how annoying people can be handing out coupons and flyers on the street. I've come to embrace this irritating scenario. Next time someone waves a flyer in your face, take it. No one likes to be rejected. That person is just doing a job, and you

can make it a little easier by simply being easygoing. You can throw it out on the next corner, or maybe you'll find you need the information after all.

3. Send a note. People don't send cards enough these days. I'm a total stationery freak, so I appreciate all kinds of paper. Send someone a personalized, handwritten note just to say hi. It will lift that person's spirits to receive a happy note and not another bill in the mail. You could also write a sweet message on a Post-it® note, and stick it on a mirror or computer monitor.

4. Listen. Sometimes people just want to be heard. I've learned that this will help you be an extraordinary friend. You don't always have to have a solution; sometimes the best remedy is just listening to someone.

5. Say thank you. When someone does something nice for you, whether in a store or a restaurant or on the street, say thank you. And really mean it. Give credit where credit is due. People like positive reinforcement.

6. Share. Lend someone your favorite book, share your favorite cookie recipe, e-mail a cute picture of a dog, tell a funny story or a joke. Spreading joy can be really simple. Start with stuff that you like. Isn't that how "Oprah's Favorite Things" came to be?

Acknowledgments

My love list:
Jay Berman

Olga Rizzo

Louis Rizzo

My teacher list:
Cathy Krein

Brenda Knight

Rita Rosenkranz

Beth Grossman

Dr. Manny Alvarez

My confidante list:
Terri Trespicio

Nicole Feldman

Lisa Logallo Chavez

Nicole Meiselbach

Carolyn Reilly

Michele Reilly

Jennifer Walsh

Jessica Mulvihill

Sharon Hazelrigg

My "brainstorming/brain picking/writing pals" list:
Jene Luciani

Emily Leibert

Erika Katz

Darcie Rowan

Mary Lengle

Shaiza Shamim

My Lists and Libations Meetup Group

My interns who helped this book come together list:
Kayla Ellman

Matthew Hauptman

Audra Martin

Isabel McCullough

Nicole Rouyer Guillet

Caitlin Scott

Erin Scott

My distractions list:

The Golden Girls

Real Simple magazine

Netflix

Pandora radio

Pretty notebooks from Papyrus, KnockKnockStuff.com, and Kate's Paperie

Pinot grigio

My inspiration list:

Oprah Winfrey

Barbara Walters

Paul T. Rizzo, my grandfather and a bookbinder for twenty-five years, who taught me to love and respect books

PAULA RIZZO is the senior health producer for FoxNews.com at Fox News Channel and the founder of ListProducer.com. She's an Emmy Award winner and attributes much of her success to her compulsive list making. The native New Yorker makes lists for every task and event she takes on, from finding an apartment to buying the perfect bra. She started ListProducer.com in April 2011 to help others become more organized, focused, efficient, and less stressed. Paula inherited her list-making skills from her father, Louis. She lives in Manhattan with her husband, Jay Berman.

TO OUR READERS

Viva Editions publishes books that inform, enlighten, and entertain. We do our best to bring you, the reader, quality books that celebrate life, inspire the mind, revive the spirit, and enhance lives all around. Our authors are practical visionaries: people who offer deep wisdom in a hopeful and helpful manner. Viva was launched with an attitude of growth and we want to spread our joy and offer our support and advice where we can to help you live the Viva way: vivaciously!

We're grateful for all our readers and want to keep bringing you books for inspired living. We invite you to write to us with your comments and suggestions, and what you'd like to see more of. You can also sign up for our online newsletter to learn about new titles, author events, and special offers.

Viva Editions
2246 Sixth St.
Berkeley, CA 94710
www.vivaeditions.com
(800) 780-2279
Follow us on Twitter @vivaeditions
Friend/fan us on Facebook